WRITERS' WORKSHOP SERIES

How to teach
writing across the curriculum
at key stage 2

SUE PALMER

David Fulton Publishers

David Fulton Publishers Ltd
Ormond House, 26-27 Boswell Street, London, WC1N 3JZ

www.fultonpublishers.co.uk

First published in Great Britain by David Fulton Publishers 2001
Reprinted 2002 (twice)

Note: the right of Sue Palmer to be identified as the author of this work has been asserted by her in accordance with the Copyright, Design and Patents Act 1998

British Library Publication Data
A catalogue record for this book is available from the British Library

ISBN 1-85346-803-7

Also available in the **Writers' Workshop Series:**

How to teach poetry writing at key stage 2   ISBN 1-85346-804-5
How to teach fiction writing at key stage 2   ISBN 1-85346-833-9

Edited by Dodi Beardshaw
Designed by Ken Vail Graphic Design
Illustrations by Martin Cater
Cover photographs by John Redman
Typeset by FiSH Books, London
Printed in Great Britain by Bell and Bain Ltd, Glasgow

Contents

Writing across the curriculum

Introduction

Writing is probably the most difficult skill teachers ever have to teach and pupils ever have to learn. This is, of course, because it isn't a single skill at all, but a vast range of skills – handwriting, phonic encoding, spelling, sentence construction, choice of vocabulary, text organisation, and many more. Each of these must be taught individually, and most of them are pretty difficult in themselves. But all the time, alongside this piecemeal learning – a snippet of one skill here, a chunk of another one there – children must learn how to blend them all together in the act of composition.

In the last few years, we have made great progress in our understanding of writing skills and the best ways to teach them. This book is based on a variety of pedagogical techniques, developed by teachers and researchers around the world, and popularised in British schools by the National Literacy Strategy (NLS) and similar initiatives in Scotland, Wales, and Ireland. The terminology used is generally the terminology adopted by the NLS.

In the teaching of non-fiction reading and writing, the current convention is to divide text into six distinct types: recount, non-chronological report, instruction, explanation, persuasion, and discussion (see page 5). While very few 'real-life' texts conform strictly to the conventions of any single text type, they provide a useful teaching vehicle for alerting children to the organisation and language features of different sorts of writing.

Much attention has been paid to helping children recognise these text types and reproduce the types of language features appropriate to each. However, if children are to write, they need some content to write about. It therefore makes sense to link the teaching of writing to what they learn in the rest of the curriculum. If children have become experts on the Spanish Armada in history, they are equipped with plenty of information to turn into recount text. If they have been learning about volcanoes in geography, they have the wherewithal to write a piece of explanation.

So far, little attention has been paid to how teachers can make clear links between writing skills and cross-curricular learning. How does one juggle the details of the subject matter and the details of teaching writing skills? This book suggests tackling writing in two discrete blocks of teaching:

1. content and organisation
2. language features.

The former provides an opportunity to survey and arrange information acquired elsewhere in the curriculum, in preparation for writing. The latter is when you concentrate on the actual composition of the piece. But you still need a way of making the initial link between cross-curricular content and the six text types: and for this we suggest using 'skeletons'.

Skeletons for writing

'Skeletons' are simple visual representations of the structures underlying written text – the skeleton frameworks upon which writing can be hung. The idea is to introduce children to these ways of organising ideas gradually by:

- demonstrating how they can be used as simple note-taking devices and aide-memoires throughout the curriculum
- teaching children how to draw them themselves, and recognise which sort of ideas and writing are associated with each skeleton
- using them to link knowledge and understanding acquired in a wide range of subject areas with the literacy skills required to record that understanding.

There are, of course, many ways to represent each text type. A **recount** could be represented by a storyboard, a flowchart, or even a numbered list. We've chosen a timeline because it's a simple, clear indicator of chronological order, and easy to remember. The simplest way to represent a **report**, on the other hand, is a spider diagram – a basic central concept from which radiates information organised into categories (in the case of the Aztecs, these might be details of homes, clothing, religion, food and farming and so on). But some reports are comparative, in which case a grid might be better. As children become familiar with the idea of skeletons, their repertoire of graphic representations can be enlarged.

    Instruction and **explanation** texts both have sequential underlying structures, for which a flowchart is an appropriate starting point, but the level of complexity will vary. This is especially the case with explanation text, which sometimes requires multiple cause–effect boxes or a cyclical structure (see page 48), or may sometimes be represented by a diagram or a sequence of diagrams. Indeed, creating graphic representations of the structures underlying individual explanation texts is an excellent way of helping children develop their understanding of cause and effect.

The six text types

Recount – retelling events, in time order

Report – describing what things are like

Instruction – how to do something

Explanation – how or why things work or happen

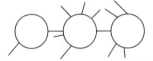

Persuasion – why you should think this

Discussion – reasoned argument

    Persuasion and **discussion** texts are different again: here we've used asterisks to represent the different points in an argument, and lines to indicate elaboration, a skeleton which has become known as 'pronged bullets'. The difference between one-sided persuasion and even-handed discussion (the for-and-against grid) is immediately obvious from the skeletons. But again, in both cases different subject matter might lead to a different visual representation.

How do skeletons work?

For over a year, I have been asking teachers on my inservice courses to try out skeletons in their classrooms, as a means of linking the teaching of writing and children's work across the curriculum. Many teachers did so and reported back. Since teachers are infinitely inventive, their reports yielded many possible uses for skeletons:

- as an aid to organising knowledge and making it more memorable (e.g. when giving a talk on an aspect of topic work)
- as a research tool and note-taking device
- as a visual, and final, means of recording what has been learned
- as a way of 'carrying' knowledge between curricular areas (e.g. from the history lesson to the Literacy Hour, to be used as the content for a piece of writing).

This final use is particularly appealing, as a means of saving time in an overcrowded curriculum – you learn about something in history, geography, or science; you write about it in English. It also opens up time for more active and varied ways of learning and recording outside literacy lessons – art, DT, drama, and speaking and listening activities.

Six case studies

A day out

*Sam Leir of The Russell School in Richmond, Surrey, asked her Year 6 class to use the **recount** skeleton to record details of an educational visit.*

"We'd been to Ham House, which dates from the time Charles II was laying out Richmond Park, and the children were given a tour of the house, followed by art, poetry and music workshops.

"When we got back we talked about the day and they devised a general skeleton with five sections: one for the tour, one for each of the three workshops, and one for the presentation they put together at the end. Then each child completed the timeline independently, depending on which workshops they'd done, and used it as a framework for writing. They added an introductory paragraph at the beginning and a concluding paragraph (what they thought about the day) at the end.

"Making the skeleton definitely improved their organisation – because of the sections they had the material sorted into paragraphs before they even thought about writing. It also helped them recognise the chronology and remember all the different events, which some children find pretty difficult! Less able writers found the whole process particularly helpful."

Intergalactic notes

*Della Williams of Oaklands Junior School in Bromley used the **report** skeleton as a research tool with her Year 6 class.*

"I gave them some information to read about the Earth, and asked them to imagine they were aliens writing a newspaper report on this new planet they'd discovered. They had to make notes on a spidergram, based on what aliens would need to know – atmospheric conditions, information about the terrain, and so on – then use them to write an article for the *Alpha Centauri Gazette*.

"They did a pretty good job, and I'm sure making the skeleton helped them internalise the information. Some of them read their articles out in assembly, and answered questions about them, and the headteacher was very impressed! It was interesting that another class who'd done the same task without a skeleton were less successful – they'd relied a lot on copying from the original text and hadn't remembered as much."

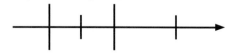

Sound practice

Jan Orman, who has a Year 5 class at Hoyland Market Street Primary School in Barnsley, used an **instruction** *skeleton to cover teaching objectives in four different curricular areas.*

"We were investigating 'Change in Sound', so it seemed a good idea to use what they'd learned to design and make simple musical instruments. I demonstrated how to draw a flowchart as a planning device, using brief notes and simple diagrams of what I intended to do. The children produced their own flowchart plans, and we photocopied them as a record of their starting point. Then they made the instruments, annotating and changing the original flowchart in a different colour as they adjusted their plans.

"After all this planning and experience, they were all pretty expert on the subject of making their musical instruments, so were ready to write instructions on how to do it. We brought our flowcharts to the Literacy Hour, and I used mine to demonstrate how to write up the stages as instructions, focusing on clear language and the use of the imperative. The children then wrote their own instructions, thus polishing off three different learning objectives with one activity. In fact, we were able to drag in a fourth – using clip art on the computer to illustrate a piece of writing!"

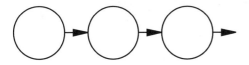

Blowing hot and cold

Caroline Andrews, Year 6 teacher at Roskear Primary School in Camborne, Cornwall, used an **explanation** *skeleton as part of her science revision.*

"In Year 6 we briefly revise all the science topics we've covered during Key Stage 2. Flowcharts, diagrams, etc. are a good way of helping children revisit and memorise the information. When we were revising solids, liquids, and gases, I made a flowchart on the board to sum up the main points – it included colour-coding (red for heat, blue for cold), simple pictures and brief notes.

"We didn't repeat the practical science work (i.e. freezing and boiling water to watch the effects), but we did do some drama to remind the children how water molecules react to being cooled or heated. They had to act the parts of the molecules: bunching up tight together when they were frozen solid, moving more freely (like water in a container) when they were liquid, and zapping about all over the place when they were heated to a gas! I think this sort of drama activity combined with a clear flowchart really aids understanding of scientific ideas.

"The dramatised revision lesson and the flowchart both came in handy when we had to cover explanation writing in the Literacy Hour. Mind you, I'm not sure whether written text is the best way to deal with explanations like this. I think children need to learn to make flowcharts and diagrams of their own, so that writing can be kept to a minimum. Clear visual representations are often much clearer."

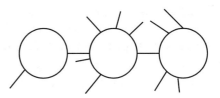

Take me home!

*Lorraine Bell, English and Drama adviser in Sutton, linked **persuasion** writing to a series of drama workshops on the Second World War.*

"We used drama to develop the children's powers of empathy and expression – the story of the evacuees is an obvious vehicle for primary children, and there's plenty of original evidence available to bring the historical facts to life. An official letter urging parents to send their children away, and a photograph of a group of people reading it, provided insights into the lifestyle of the time and a stimulus for role play. Children took the parts of characters in the photo, arguing different points of view, especially those of the prospective evacuees. A 'packing list' of what evacuees should take with them became the basis of further role play. Pairs of pupils became parent and child, working through the list, pondering on what was going to happen. By this time, many children were identifying strongly with the evacuees and their anxiety.

"We also studied photos of children being waved off at the station, or sitting on the train to create living tableaux with opportunities for 'characters' to voice their feelings. I also read some extracts about children's experiences on arrival – waiting to be chosen or, even worse, not being chosen at all. By this time, the class was immersed in what it was like to be an evacuee, so we asked them to do more role play – arguing the case for staying in the country or going back home.

"After all this first-hand experience, it was easy to make notes on a persuasion skeleton for a letter to the officials who'd sent them to the country – either pleading to go home or commending the evacuation programme. They later wrote up the letters to put in their project folders."

Fuelling discussion

*Amanda Hulme of St Bede's CE Primary in Bolton is an enthusiastic and innovative skeleton user. Her Year 4 class had formed a human timeline in preparation for writing on the Tudors, and used a spidergram to record findings in geography, so she was ready to exploit this opportunity for **discussion**.*

"We got talking about fuel protesters during an 'In the news' session, and the children had quite strong feelings on one side or another. Since they were pretty used to skeletons by this time, I quickly doled out a for-and-against grid and asked them to note – very briefly – some of the main arguments on each side.

"In Literacy Hour we looked at examples of balanced discussions, and created a simple writing frame about our topic. Most of the class were able to draft their writing on the frame while I helped the poorest group. Then people read samples of their drafts and we talked about the phrasing, and whether it sounded formal enough – like a news broadcast.

"I really like the skeletons, because – quite apart from helping the children organise their writing – they help me make connections between the text types and what I'm doing in the rest of the curriculum. Now I'm used to them, I can see straight away whether a particular topic will make a report, recount, explanation or whatever. I think they're much more than a writing tool – over time they'll develop the children's thinking skills as well."

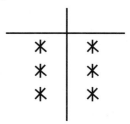

An edited version of these case studies first appeared in TES *Primary* magazine in March 2001.

Activities for speaking and listening

What all these case studies have in common is an emphasis on children's first-hand experiences and opportunities for talk. As both common sense and educational research tell us, these two elements underpin knowledge and understanding, and without them our pupils simply have nothing to write about.

Speaking and listening activities are therefore critical to successful writing. These include constant opportunities for:

- focused spoken language activities in pairs or groups
- delivering prepared talks or presentations to the class or a school assembly
- regular role-play and drama activities
- 'class talk' – i.e. opportunities for interaction between teacher and pupils – in all shared lessons throughout the curriculum.

The activities suggested on the following pages are linked to various skeleton frameworks, but most can be adapted to work in many areas.

Skeleton notes may be created on computer. Group work of this kind provides a context for highly-focused speaking and listening

Recount

Retelling

- Using brief notes/pictures on a timeline as a prompt, select pupils to retell a short section each to the class.
- Ask pupils in pairs to retell it to each other, taking alternate paragraphs (see Key Teaching Points, page 16).

Dramatisation

- You retell the story, stopping off at particular points and asking the class, in pairs or groups, to take on the roles of characters and enact an incident. **Role-play retelling** is greatly enhanced if you also sometimes take on a role.

- Ask groups to dramatise significant sections of the story, to re-enact for the class. These dramatisations can be presented as **mini-plays**, or as mimed reconstructions, for which one pupil from the group provides a commentary.
- Stage a **puppet play** of the story, based on the timeline (or a number of mini-puppet plays, each produced by a group). Puppeteers can improvise lines for this, or a narrator can tell the story as the puppets perform.
- Ask groups to **freeze-frame** critical moments from the timeline, i.e. create a living tableau from which participants are invited to step out, and comment on their own part in it.

Instruction

Do-it-yourself

The best way to familiarise oneself with the content of instructions is actually to carry out the process. If pupils write with a partner, they can talk through the process to create skeleton notes on a flowchart as they go along.

Dramatised demonstrations

- Ask a pupil (or group) to prepare a **TV demonstration**, à la Delia Smith or Tony Hart, demonstrating the process. Others watch, then question to create a flowchart of the steps.
- For instructions such as road safety rules, stage a **mimed demonstration with commentary**, presented like a public service advertisement.
- Try the same activity using **puppets**.

Report

Prepared talks

- Children often find it easier to plan and deliver a talk using spidergram notes than traditional linear notes. **Illustrated talks** are the most successful, so encourage them also to prepare props, such as pictures or artefacts (home-made or collected).

- Set up a **Brains Trust**, so that pupils can share knowledge researched as individuals or in pairs. Each pupil/pair, with spidergram notes as a prompt, takes turns to give a brief talk then answer questions.
- Ask groups to organise **TV** or **radio documentaries** about subjects they have researched, including commentary, interviews, and, where appropriate, mini-dramatisations.

Explanation

Physical theatre

Turn the process to be explained into **imaginative role play**, as in the case study on page 7. With a little imagination, you can transform pupils into particles, planets, blood corpuscles, animals in a food chain, parts of a plant...Organising physical theatre is fun and helps everyone involved recognise the critical points in a process, which helps in composing a flowchart.

Illustrated talks

Once pupils have created flowchart skeletons or diagrams of a process, use them as a focus for speaking and listening. As a pupil/pair explains their skeleton, the rest of the class listens and questions. At the end, the class selects the best skeleton, or creates a composite.

Persuasion

Drama activities

Drama helps engage children emotionally with the subject before they write persuasive text, as illustrated in the case study 'Take me home!' on page 8.

- Adapt the suggestions for **dramatisation** given under 'Recount' to fit your subject matter, giving pupils opportunities to empathise with the characters concerned.
- Put pupils into the role of significant players, then put them in the **hot seat** to answer questions about their part in events from the rest of the class.
- Use **mime** and **dance** activities to help children think themselves into a subject, e.g. play 'Mars' from Holst's orchestral suite *The Planets* and ask groups to create a mime/dance about the destruction of an animal habitat.

Broadcasts

- Ask groups of pupils to devise a **TV** or **radio advertisement** for a product or point of view, based on their 'pronged bullet' skeleton.
- Watch a video of **party political broadcasts** (available from *www.politicos.co.uk*), then ask pupils to use skeleton notes to devise their own broadcast, on behalf of whatever pressure group they wish to represent.

Discussion

Debates

- Use a for-and-against skeleton as the basis of a **formal debate**, with a speaker (and seconder) for and against the motion, followed by contributions from the floor (everyone else). Allow time for the two speakers to sum up their cases before taking a vote.

- Stage your own version of **Question Time**, with one or two children taking the roles of characters strongly pro and anti a particular issue. Invite questions and comments from the floor, so the activity becomes a sort of 'dual hot-seating'.

Cross-curricular links

There are innumerable occasions across the curriculum when a particular text type (and its related skeleton) is appropriate to a particular chunk of learning. Once pupils are aware of the six text types and their skeletons, it is always useful to discuss the appropriate way to record or write up a piece of work – and, if possible, make skeleton notes – whether you intend pupils to write it up or not. Awareness of the underlying structure aids retention of the information.

Recount

'True stories' to be told in chronological order are probably the most common themes for writing in a variety of areas, for example:

- PHSE: pupils' own news, anecdotes, or personal accounts
- General: accounts of schoolwork, sporting events, or outings
- History: accounts of historical events
- RE: stories from the great religions
- History, RE, Art, Music: biographical writing.

Report

Learning based on a recognition of the characteristics of something includes:

- History: describing any aspect of daily life in any historical period, e.g. fashion, transport, buildings, or food
- Science: describing the characteristics of anything, e.g. particular plants or animals; the various planets in the solar system; or different sorts of rock or material
- Geography: describing and comparing localities or geographical features
- RE: describing the characteristics of religions and the lifestyles of religious groups
- PHSE: describing the life, work or activities of any group of people.

Instruction

There are many occasions across the curriculum when children carry out activities which can become the content for writing instructions, for example:

- Design and Technology: how to design and make an artefact
- ICT: how to operate the computer
- Art: how to carry out a particular art activity
- Science: how to carry out an experiment
- PE: how to play a team game or carry out an activity
- PHSE: rules for behaviour, e.g. in school, hygiene or road safety
- Maths: how to carry out a mathematical procedure.

Links to QCA schemes of work

Teachers using the QCA schemes of work for History, Geography, Science, Religious Education, and Design and Technology can find links between the existing writing activities and NLS objectives on the QCA website (*www.qca.org.uk*).

Explanation

Questions of 'how' and 'why' arise in all subject areas, and the creation of flowcharts and diagrams can be invaluable in understanding them, for example:

- Science: explaining electricity, forces, the seasons, insulation, food chains or the life cycles of plants and animals
- History: explaining inventions like the steam engine; the causes of historical events such as wars and revolutions; or the role of the Nile in determining the seasons of Ancient Egypt
- Geography: explaining meteorological phenomena, e.g. the water cycle or global warming; physical phenomena, e.g. how a volcano erupts or how rocks are eroded
- RE: explaining religious traditions and practices (this often becomes confused with recount: see box below).

Persuasion

In order to write persuasion text, pupils must be knowledgeable about the subject concerned. Topics for persuasive writing may arise from many aspects of work across the curriculum, for example:

- History: publicity campaigns or brochures based on local history studies or on trips to museums and places of interest; editorials or letters to the editor on controversial issues in any period of history (see sample text on page 57)
- Geography: letter-writing on topics 'In the news' such as 'Should the High Street be closed to traffic?' and other local, national, and international issues, from deforestation to global warming
- PHSE and Citizenship: poster and leaflet campaigns about bullying, road safety, stranger danger, or substance abuse
- Science: posters, articles and leaflets promoting a healthy lifestyle based on science work about teeth or nutrition.

Discussion

Debates and discussion writing arise from controversies in a variety of subject areas, including:

- History: historical attitudes to gender, race, children, class or colonialism, which could be discussed in editorials
- Geography: pollution, transport policy, land use or deforestation
- Science: GM foods, factory farming, vegetarianism or space exploration
- PHSE: smoking, bullying, divorce, or television programmes
- Art, Music, Literature: opinions on particular works.

Combined text types

Very often, one piece of writing requires a combination of text types. An account of Christmas traditions, for instance, will probably involve report text to describe the tradition, then change to recount or explanation (or a mixture of both) to explain its origin. Children should be aware that the text types are essentially teaching and learning tools, and that real life doesn't always slot so readily into neat categories.

A teaching plan

Select your teaching objective

Select text type from grid opposite, then see year-by-year teaching pages

Read examples of the text type

Draw attention to:

– audience and purpose

– organisation

– language features

Example texts with analysis of purpose, organisation and language features

List of suitable Big Books

Anthologies of example texts

Choose content to write about

– draw this from any relevant area of the curriculum

– ensure children's understanding through various activities, e.g. speaking and listening drama and role-play art, craft, music

Cross-curricular links

Activities for speaking and listening

Display your objectives

Ensure pupils are clear about your teaching objectives at each stage. *Skeleton Poster Books*, one for each text type (see 'other materials', page 79) provide a range of simple, large-print posters covering each aspect mentioned in the chart above.

Organise information in a 'skeleton' format

Skeletons for writing

page 5

Sample skeletons

Recount   pages 18, 22
Report   pages 30, 34
Instruction   page 42
Explanation page 50
Persuasion   page 58
Discussion   page 66

Teach about language features of the genre

– teach sentence-level work as appropriate
– demonstrate in shared writing

NLS sentence-level links on year-by-year teaching pages

Recount   pages 24–7
Report   pages 36–9
Instruction   pages 44–7
Explanation pages 52–5
Persuasion   pages 60–62
Discussion   page 68

Shared writing

pages 74–5

Teach about purpose and organisation of writing

– define audience and purpose for writing
– choose text type
– design layout

Purpose + audience → form and style

pages 70–73

Recommended books and resources

page 79

Provide independent writing task

– scaffold as appropriate for different groups
– work with one guided group
– revisit objectives in plenary session

Independent and guided writing

page 76

Planning and plenary

page 77

Term by term planning grid				
	Year 3	**Year 4**	**Year 5**	**Year 6**
Term 1	Recount Report	Recount Instruction Report	Recount Instruction	Recount Report
Term 2	Instruction	Explanation	Report Explanation	Persuasion Discussion
Term 3	Recount	Persuasion	Persuasion	Discussion All text types

Unit 1 – Recount text

Personal recounts

Purpose: to retell events (from the point of view of someone who was there).

Example: first-person account of a school trip, written like a 'news' piece.

Text structure

- orientation: setting the scene – who, what, when, where?
- sequential organisation – what happened, in time order
- closing statement(s) – bringing the writing to a satisfactory conclusion
- basic skeleton framework – a **timeline** ('this happened, then this happened, etc.').

Language features

- past tense (specific events that only happened once)
- time connectives and other devices to aid chronological structure
- first-person writing
- focus on specific participants, including writer.

Key teaching points

- Personal recount text is clearly related to the traditional '**news** writing', common throughout primary school. It is therefore sometimes considered one of the easiest types of non-fiction writing.

- However, personal recount covers a range of different types of text, from the informal, subjective writing in personal diaries and letters to the formal, objective writing-up of a science experiment. The issue of **purpose** and **audience** is often particularly significant in the writing of personal recounts.

- Many children also need considerable help in organising information into **chronological order**. If facts or experiences are new to them, they often omit or confuse events. Preliminary organisation on a timeline can help children recall information and see its place in the overall sequence of events.

- The completed timeline may also be used as a paragraph planner. Before writing, pupils can draw lines across the timeline to designate appropriate paragraph breaks.

Common forms of personal recount text
- letter
- autobiography
- diary or journal
- newspaper report
- magazine article
- write-up of a trip or activity
- account of a science experiment

Big book examples of personal recount text

My Holiday Diary Heinemann Discovery World

Historical Letters and Diaries Longman Pelican

Extracts from Zlata's Diary Heinemann Literacy World Stage 3 NF Big Book A

See also 'Recommended books for teachers' on pages 79–80.

A trip to the Eden Project

Last Friday, our class travelled in the school bus to visit the Eden Project in Cornwall. It was a long ride to get there so we had to be at school an hour early, at eight o'clock. We brought our breakfast to eat on the bus.

When we arrived at the Eden Project, we could tell it was a big attraction by the size of the car parks, which were carefully laid out and named after fruits – we were in Plum Car Park. As we walked down, we could see the Eden Project buildings – two enormous plastic domes, built in a dip in the ground.

Mrs Jeffries told us they were called 'biomes' and the dip used to be a claypit, where men had dug out the clay to use for making pots. We spent our morning going round the biomes, looking at the plants. One is kept very warm inside and filled with tropical plants like rubber trees, bamboo, spices, coconuts and pineapples. There are also displays of buildings and gardens from tropical countries. The other biome is not so warm and among the plants there are oranges, lemons, grapes and olives.

We had our lunch in the exhibition centre, where we watched a video about 'The making of Eden'. The Eden Project was built to show how men and plants depend upon each other and it cost millions of pounds to build. Next we had a talk about the plants. A lady explained how you get cocoa beans and cocoa milk from a pod and use them to make chocolate.

We were allowed to look in the shop and spend two pounds. I bought some stickers and a postcard of a man building the biomes. Finally, it was time for the long ride home. We were back by half past three, just in time for the bell.

Audience
Readers who know the writer, or at least are familiar with his or her background.

Purpose
1. to recount the events of a significant day (a school trip)
2. to provide objective factual information about the Eden Project.

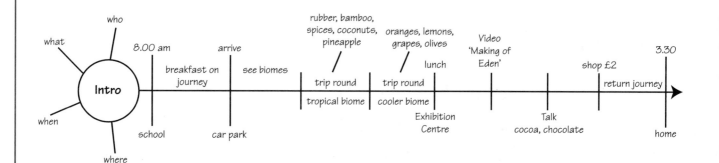

what

who

8.00 am   arrive   rubber, bamboo, spices, coconuts, pineapple   oranges, lemons, grapes, olives   Video 'Making of Eden'   3.30

breakfast on journey   see biomes   trip round tropical biome   lunch   shop £2

Intro   trip round cooler biome   return journey

when   Exhibition Centre   Talk cocoa, chocolate

where   school   car park   home

Organisation and content

Title: straightforward summary of content to follow.

Introduction

Paragraph 1: details of
  who (our class)
  what (trip to Eden Project)
  when (last Friday, setting off early)
  where (in Cornwall).

Recount

The outward journey is dealt with in paragraph 1.

Paragraph 2: arrival at the Eden Project and first impressions.

Paragraph 3: the tour of the biomes (including information on the building of the Eden Project).

Paragraph 4: lunch and the afternoon's events (including information on the purpose of the Eden Project).

Conclusion

Final paragraph: the end of the trip, return journey and arrival home.

A trip to the Eden Project

Last Friday, our class travelled in the school bus to visit the Eden Project in Cornwall. It was a long ride to get there so we had to be at school an hour early, at eight o'clock. We brought our breakfast to eat on the bus.

When we arrived at the Eden Project, we could tell it was a big attraction by the size of the car parks, which were carefully laid out and named after fruits – we were in Plum Car Park. As we walked down, we could see the Eden Project buildings – two enormous plastic domes, built in a dip in the ground.

Mrs Jeffries told us they were called 'biomes' and the dip used to be a claypit, where men had dug out the clay to use for making pots. We spent our morning going round the biomes, looking at the plants. One is kept very warm inside and filled with tropical plants like rubber trees, bamboo, spices, coconuts and pineapples. There are also displays of buildings and gardens from tropical countries. The other biome is not so warm and among the plants there are oranges, lemons, grapes and olives.

We had our lunch in the exhibition centre, where we watched a video about 'The making of Eden'. The Eden Project was built to show how men and plants depend upon each other and it cost millions of pounds to build. Next we had a talk about the plants. A lady explained how you get cocoa beans and cocoa milk from a pod and use them to make chocolate.

We were allowed to look in the shop and spend two pounds. I bought some stickers and a postcard of a man building the biomes. Finally, it was time for the long ride home. We were back by half past three, just in time for the bell.

How to teach writing across the curriculum at key stage 2 © Sue Palmer   17

Form and style

- personal recount text – an account in diary format
- events in chronological order
- significant detail, including examples, as personally recalled
- objective, factual description.

Language features

Specific language

- Mostly written in the **past tense** because the trip was a specific event, which only happened once. However, the third paragraph, describing the project, is mainly in the **present tense** because the information is general: the things described continue to exist once the trip is over.
- **Specific participants** (*our class*).

Personal language

- Written in the **first person** (mostly plural, *our class* and *we*, but with a singular reference, *I*, in the final paragraph).
- The writer assumes a high level of background knowledge on behalf of the reader (references to *last Friday, our class, school, Mrs Jeffries*).
- Despite the personal language, however, this is a highly objective account (see 'Informative language' below).

Time and sequence

- Exact timings for the **beginning** and **end** of the excursion help establish that time is an important element in this chronological account (*Last Friday . . . at school an hour early, at eight o'clock; half past three, just in time for the bell*).

- **Paragraphing** helps clarify timing: each paragraph deals with a well-defined section of the day (see 'Organisation and content' opposite)
- **Sequential connectives** to open sentences (*When..., As..., Next..., Finally...*) help to indicate the sequence of events.

Informative language

While the account is a personal one, it is objective rather than subjective. The author recounts what happened on the trip, but makes no personal comments or value judgements. There is no attempt to engage or excite the reader.

- Basic **verbs** (*get, brought, arrived, walked*, etc.).
- Descriptive language (**adjectives** and **adverbs**) provide factual detail, rather than effect (*a long ride, a big attraction, enormous plastic domes, very warm, not so warm*).
- Description sometimes based on logical **deduction** (*we could tell it was a big attraction by the size of the car parks*).
- Provision of **examples** (*tropical plants like...; among the plants there are...*).
- Emphasis on **sources of information/evidence** (*we could see...; Mrs Jeffries told us...; we watched a video...; we had a talk...; a lady explained how...*).

Impersonal recounts

Purpose: to retell events (from an impersonal standpoint).

Example: third-person account of a school outing, written as a magazine article.

Text structure

- orientation: setting the scene – who, what, when, where?
- sequential organisation – what happened, in time order
- closing statement(s) – bringing the writing to a satisfactory conclusion
- basic skeleton framework – a **timeline** ('this happened, then this happened, etc.').

Language features

- past tense (specific events that only happened once)
- time connectives and other devices to aid chronological structure
- third-person writing
- focus on specific participants (named individuals/groups).

Key teaching points

- Impersonal recount text clearly shares many characteristics with **narrative** writing, and is therefore sometimes considered one of the easiest types of non-fiction writing.

- However, impersonal recount covers a range of different types of writing, from informal, subjective, value-laden accounts in magazines to the formal, objective writing of a scientific report. The issue of **purpose** and **audience** is often particularly significant in the writing of impersonal recounts.

- Many children also need considerable help in organising information into **chronological order**. Preliminary organisation of the information on a timeline can help children recall information and see its place in the overall sequence of events.

- The completed timeline may also be used as a paragraph planner. Before writing, pupils can draw lines across the timeline to designate appropriate paragraph breaks.

Common forms of personal recount text
- non-fiction book (e.g. history)
- biography
- magazine article
- newspaper report
- encyclopedia entry
- obituary
- account of science experiment.

Big book examples of impersonal recount text

The First Lunar Landing Rigby Magic Bean

Elizabeth 1/St Francis/Guy Fawkes/Mother Teresa Heinemann Library (Life and Times)

Alan Shearer: a biography Heinemann Literacy World Stage 4 NF Big Book A

See also anthologies on page 80.

A taste of Paradise

"All this way to see plants in a greenhouse!" After two hours watching rain stream by the bus windows on the long road to Cornwall last Friday, Year 5 was feeling less than enthusiastic about visiting the Eden Project. Yet as the children made their way across the vast car parks, catching their first glimpse of two huge plastic 'biomes' in a gigantic crater, they began to change their minds.

The Eden Project is the largest greenhouse in the world, big enough to hold the Tower of London and housing more than 135,000 plants. In the humid tropical biome, Year 5 found themselves wandering through a South American rainforest, basking in a Polynesian garden, sighing in the stifling heat beside a tropical waterfall. They saw plants they knew – bananas, pineapples, mangoes, cocoa, rice – not picked and packaged on supermarket shelves, but alive and growing. They saw plants they didn't know and hadn't dreamed of. They began to realise how much human beings depend on nature for all their basic needs – food, drink, shelter, clothing – and luxuries – sweets, cosmetics, sports gear…

In the warm temperate biome, the heat was gentler and the air filled with the scent of lemons. Here they saw the plants of California and the Mediterranean: olives, vines, tobacco, cotton, cork and mouth-watering fruit and vegetables. Outside, on the slopes leading up to the exhibition hall, were the familiar plants of the cool temperate zone, and the familiar weather – still raining!

After lunch, there was a film about the building of Eden and a talk from the education department… and then the long drive home. But now as the rain beat down and the windows steamed up, Year 5 could close their eyes and remember Paradise. The scents of jasmine, ginger and pineapple; the sultry tropical heat; the rainbow colours of wild, exotic flowers. Some plants; some greenhouse!

Audience

Readers of a school magazine or newspaper (pupils, parents, governors – many of them unknown to the writer).

Purpose

1. to recount the events of a significant day (a school trip)
2. to provide factual information about the Eden Project
3. to engage and entertain the reader.

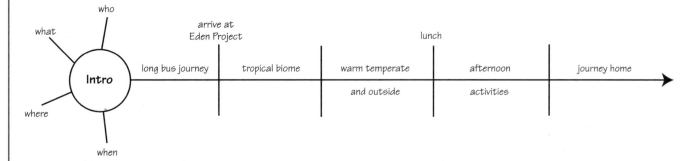

Organisation and content

Title: Eye-catching title to attract attention: quote from Bounty advert; play on words (Eden/Paradise).

Introduction

Paragraph 1: details of
  who (our class)
  what (trip to Eden Project)
  when (last Friday)
  where (in Cornwall)

Establishes atmosphere of a rainy coach ride, negative feelings (especially negative opening line). On arrival at Eden Project, change of tone – positive.

Events in chronological order

The outward journey and arrival at the Eden Project are dealt with in paragraph 1.

Paragraph 2: upbeat, factual information about Eden Project. Evocative description of trip round tropical biome. Final sentence sums up Eden Project's message (interdependence of humans and plants).

Paragraph 3: evocative description of trip round warm temperate biome. Brief description of outside zone – "still raining" contrasts with the lushness of the biomes.

Conclusion

Paragraph 4: summary of the afternoon's events.Return journey – returns to theme of wet coach ride, but with positive slant. Final line is a riposte to the negative opening.

A taste of Paradise

"All this way to see plants in a greenhouse!" After two hours watching rain stream by the bus windows on the long road to Cornwall last Friday, Year 5 was feeling less than enthusiastic about visiting the Eden Project. Yet as the children made their way across the vast car parks, catching their first glimpse of two huge plastic 'biomes' in a gigantic crater, they began to change their minds.

The Eden Project is the largest greenhouse in the world, big enough to hold the Tower of London and housing more than 135,000 plants. In the humid tropical biome, Year 5 found themselves wandering through a South American rainforest, basking in a Polynesian garden, sighing in the stifling heat beside a tropical waterfall. They saw plants they knew – bananas, pineapples, mangoes, cocoa, rice – not picked and packaged on supermarket shelves, but alive and growing. They saw plants they didn't know and hadn't dreamed of. They began to realise how much human beings depend on nature for all their basic needs – food, drink, shelter, clothing – and luxuries – sweets, cosmetics, sports gear…

In the warm temperate biome, the heat was gentler and the air filled with the scent of lemons. Here they saw the plants of California and the Mediterranean: olives, vines, tobacco, cotton, cork and mouth-watering fruit and vegetables. Outside, on the slopes leading up to the exhibition hall, were the familiar plants of the cool temperate zone, and the familiar weather – still raining!

After lunch, there was a film about the building of Eden and a talk from the education department… and then the long drive home. But now as the rain beat down and the windows steamed up, Year 5 could close their eyes and remember Paradise. The scents of jasmine, ginger and pineapple; the sultry tropical heat; the rainbow colours of wild, exotic flowers. Some plants; some greenhouse!

Form and style

- third-person recount text – a magazine feature
- events in chronological order
- significant detail, including examples
- descriptive, engaging writing style.

Language features

Specific language

- Mostly written in the **past tense** because the trip was a specific event, which only happened once. However, the opening of paragraph 2, describing the project is in the **present tense** because the information is general: the things described continue to exist once the trip is over.
- **Specific participants** (*Year 5*).

Impersonal language

- Written in the **third person** (mostly plural, *Year 5* and *the children*). We do not know who the author is – could be a member of Year 5, the teacher, an accompanying reporter...
- Despite the impersonal stance, however, this is a highly subjective account (see 'Use of language' below).

Time and sequence

- **Paragraphing** helps clarify timing: each paragraph deals with a well-defined section of the day (see 'Organisation' opposite).
- **Sequential connectives** to open sentences (*After two hours... After lunch...*) help to indicate the sequence of events, but most of the chronology is carried in the layout.

Use of language to engage and entertain

While this recount provides much the same information as the first example, the use of language is much more subjective – it has been carefully chosen to engage the reader, and to persuade him or her of the attractions of the Eden Project (see also 'Persuasion text' on pages 56–63).

- **Direct speech** for opening line draws reader in.
- Descriptive language including **powerful verbs** (*wandering, basking, sighing,* etc.) and **adjectives** (*stifling, mouth-watering, sultry, tropical, wild, exotic*).
- Frequent use of **lists** to suggest lushness and plenty (lists of plants, plant uses, memories through different senses on the trip home).
- Use of **repetition** for effect (*They saw plants they knew...They saw plants they didn't know; familiar plants...familiar weather*).
- **Alliteration** (*picked and packaged; jasmine, ginger*).
- Use of **contrast** (the rainy journey contrasted with the tropical heat; the children's negative feelings on the way, contrasted with their changed outlook on the way back).
- **Variety of sentence construction**. In paragraph 2, a repeated sentence construction (*They saw...They saw...They began to realise...*) creates a cumulative effect. In paragraph 3, sentences open with adverbials of place (*In the warm temperate biome...Here...Outside...*).
- Use of **connectives** to create contrast. In both the first and final paragraph the key effect is a contrast (negative rainy journey/positive Eden Project). Both these hinge on a connective (paragraph 1's *Yet...*; paragraph 4's *But...*). The tone of the writing on either side of the connective is very different.

Year 3 recount writing

NLS text-level references

T1 reading: 17, 18, 21, non-fiction text structures and key facts

T1 writing: 22, recording information from texts read

T3 writing: 22, recounting the same event in a variety of ways.

NLS sentence-level links

T1: writing in sentences, verbs, and tense

T2: use of adjectives, first and third person verbs

T3: sequential connectives, first and third person pronouns.

Content and organisation

Focus on chronological order. Help children recognise how events are sequenced and how they can be represented in skeleton form by:

- converting the information in a recount text into brief notes on a timeline (see examples on pages 18 and 22)
- creating timelines for events studied in history or other subjects, either from your teaching or by compiling information from a number of sources
- creating timeline records of school events, such as outings.

Language features

- Verbs and tense: stress the past tense by using it on timeline notes. (This doesn't come naturally – it's more obvious to write notes in the present tense, which leads some children to wander into the present when writing their recounts).
- Powerful verbs, adjectives: these are important features of vivid recount writing. Demonstrate how to select appropriate ones during shared writing.
- Sequential connectives: collect examples from reading and display on a poster.
- First and third person: illustrate with the sample recounts or other suitable texts.

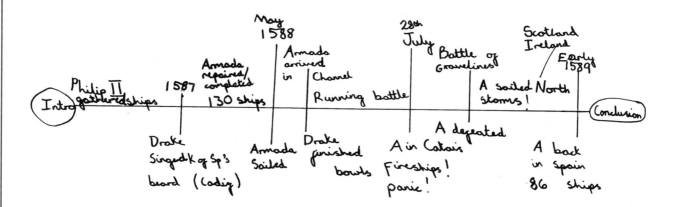

Making timelines

- Make a rough timeline first (this can be a useful way of familiarising yourself with the information to be taught, and may be used as lesson notes).

- Create timelines for class use in a variety of ways, e.g.
  - a large timeline on a roll of wallpaper
  - a human timeline: write events on cards and give to children to organise themselves in appropriate order
  - a washing timeline: write events on cards and peg along a washing line.

- Don't worry about exact time markings: just generally link length of time to distance along line.

- Use vertical lines to note specific events; write ongoing events along the line.

Year 4 recount writing

NLS text-level references

T1 reading: 18, opening sentences that set scenes; 20, features of newspapers

T1 writing: 24, writing newspaper-style reports of events

T2 writing: 21, making short notes.

NLS sentence-level links

T1: verbs and tense, powerful verbs, adverbs

T2: use of adjectives, significance of word order.

Content and organisation

Continue to focus on chronological order (see Year 3).

- As a note-taking activity, ask pupils to create brief timeline notes of familiar events such as the school day, or what they did at the weekend or during a holiday.
- Occasionally ask a child to make notes on a class activity, e.g. when someone is unable to take part in gym or games, ask him or her to take notes of the main events of the lesson and use them to create a timeline.
- As a class, take brief notes on the content of a television programme and arrange as a timeline.

Any of these timeline skeletons may be used as the basis of a piece of recount writing.

Language features

- Powerful verbs, adjectives, adverbs: these are important for engaging and entertaining your audience when writing newspaper-type reports. Compare the effectiveness of our two examples analysed on pages 18–19 (basic verbs, factual adjectives) and pages 22–3 (powerful verbs, vivid adjectives).
- Word order: this can be covered when working on writing an introductory paragraph (see below). Concentrate on the first four questions in the box. Demonstrate how to summarise the key facts in a couple of sentences, by making very brief notes in response to each question. Show how these facts can be linked together and turned into complete sentences. Encourage pupils to try a variety of different ways of crafting the opening sentences – use a mixture of oral work, scribing, and supported writing (see pages 74–5).

Writing an introductory paragraph

Newspaper reports should always answer these key questions in their opening paragraph:

who is it about?
what happened?
when did it happen?
where did it happen?
why should my reader bother to find out more?

The first four questions provide basic background information which orientates the reader, and makes the subsequent text easier to follow. The final question is about 'hooking' the reader's attention. This is actually a good formula for the opening paragraph of any recount piece.

WHO?
Philip II of Spain
Elizabeth I of England

WHAT?
Spanish Armada (130 ships) defeated

WHY IS IT interesting?
Defeat of huge fleet that seemed invincible

WHEN?
1588

WHERE?
English Channel

Year 5 recount writing

NLS text-level references

T1 reading: 21, features of recounted texts;
23, types of note-taking

T1 writing: 24, recounts for different audiences;
26, notes for different purposes.

NLS sentence-level links

T1: writing for different audiences and purposes; direct and reported speech; reordering sentences.

Content and organisation

Focus on paragraphing.

- In reading recounts, note how the author has decided on paragraph breaks, e.g. in our first example text, ask pupils to summarise the content of each paragraph.
- Continue work on chronological order (see Years 3 and 4). Expect pupils to create timeline notes for themselves in history and other subjects.
- Use timeline notes from other curricular areas as a basis for recount writing. Before writing, discuss the best way to divide the information on the timeline into paragraphs.
- Draw vertical coloured lines through the timeline to show where the paragraph breaks will come. Use these as a guide when writing.

Language features

- Writing for different audiences and purposes:
  - Personal versus impersonal writing: illustrate the difference with our examples or other suitable texts. Look for further examples. Discuss which might be more appropriate for various audiences, e.g. young children, university experts, magazine readers, people looking up information in an encyclopadia.
  - Subjective versus objective writing: illustrate with our examples or other suitable texts and look for further examples. Discuss which might be more appropriate for various audiences, as above.
- Reported and direct speech:
  - reported speech can be quicker and can gloss over details, e.g. in the first example text, *Mrs Jeffries told us ... A lady explained how ...* Investigate the construction, tense (always past), and person (third). Try changing to direct speech.
  - direct speech (a direct quotation) can be used in non-fiction writing for effect: it's more immediately impactful and vivid, e.g. the opening line of the second example text.

Reordering sentences

Choose suitable sentences from recount text to cut up into chunks and write on cards. Pupils should hold these to make a human sentence, or you can peg them on a washing line. Try reorganising them in various ways to see if the meaning is altered, or the rhythm or emphasis can be improved. In the first example text, try:

| Last Friday | our class | travelled | in the school bus | to visit the Eden Project | in Cornwall. |

| As we walked down | we could see | the Eden Project buildings | two enormous plastic domes |

| built in a dip in the ground. |

On the whole, you'll find it's adverbial chunks (answering the questions *when*, *where*, and *how*) that can be moved around most easily. The choice of chunk with which you open the sentence affects the emphasis. Word order also has an effect on punctuation.

Year 6 recount writing

NLS text-level references

T1 reading: 11, biography and autobiography
T1 writing: 14, biographical and auto-biographical writing;
15, 16 journalistic style
T3 reading: 19, review a range of text types
T3 writing: 22, select appropriate style and form for purpose and audience.

NLS sentence-level links

T1: connecting words and phrases; complex sentences
T3: language conventions of recounts.

Content and organisation

- Give children blank timelines divided into twelve equal sections (one per year) and ask them to make autobiographical timelines for homework. Suggest they illustrate these with photographs and other documentation.
- On the basis of the timeline, ask children to design an autobiographical booklet, with a number of short chapters, in which the photos, etc. can be interpolated as the text is written.
- When studying famous people in history, RE, etc., make biographical timelines. Divide into paragraphs (see work on pages 25 and 26) and use as the basis for biographical writing.

Language features

- Writing an Introductory paragraph: revise Year 4 work (see page 25), adding that in biographical writing the opening should also sum up, or give a clue to, why the subject was famous.
- Connecting words and phrases; complex sentences: collect examples of effective words, phrases and sentence constructions from reading of biographies and display on a wall poster for pupils to use when they are writing.

Recount checklist

Organisation

- Does the introductory paragraph answer the questions *who, what, when, where* so that the reader has a rough idea of what the piece will be about? ❏
- Does the introductory paragraph also draw the reader in by suggesting why the topic is worth reading about (or, in the case of biography, why the subject became famous)? ❏
- Is the recount in clear chronological order? ❏
- Is this supported by the positioning of paragraph breaks? ❏
- Is there a closing statement, bringing the timeline to a satisfactory conclusion? ❏

Language features

- Is the text consistently in the past tense (except for references to places/circumstances which are ongoing)? ❏
- Is the text consistently in the first person or third person, depending on whether it is a personal or impersonal recount? ❏
- Does the text use vocabulary and sentence structures appropriate to the audience? ❏
- Are there time connectives and other devices to aid the chronological structure? ❏

Unit 2 – Report text

Non-comparative reports

Purpose: to describe the characteristics of something.

Example: an extract from a general encyclopedia.

Text structure

- introductory information about what is to be described: who, what, when, where? (overall classification)
- non-chronological organisation
- description organised according to categories of information
- basic skeleton framework – a **spidergram** (one spider leg per category, which could divide into further spider legs, depending on degree of detail).

Language features

- present tense (except historical reports)
- usually general nouns and pronouns (not particular people or things)
- third person writing
- factual writing, often involving technical words and phrases.

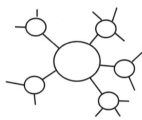

Key teaching points

- Non-comparative report text deals with a single topic, which may be wide-ranging, e.g. 'Ancient Greece' or 'Birds', or more focused, e.g. 'The Scottish wildcat'.

- The difference between report and recount is that report text is usually non-chronological. The basic skeletons for the two text types show this difference clearly.

- Learning to organise report text involves learning to categorise information. There are three stages in making a spidergram (see 'How to BOS' on page 37), and many children find the process challenging. It is, however, worth the effort to teach it well, as categorisation is an important thinking skill.

- There are other ways of representing report text (e.g. a picture, labelled diagram, plan or map) which may be used instead of or in addition to the spidergram.

Common forms of non-comparative report text
- information leaflet
- school-project file
- tourist guidebook
- encyclopedia entry
- magazine article
- non-fiction book (e.g. geography)
- letter.

Big book examples of non-comparative report text
The Moon Kingscourt

The Sun Kingscourt

Looking After the Egg Ginn (All Aboard)

My Christian/Hindu/Muslim Faith Evans

School by a Volcano Longman Book Project

Victorian Clothes Longman Book Project

See also 'Recommended books for teachers' on pages 79–80.

Butterflies

Butterflies belong to the order of insects known as Lepidoptera. This means they have scaly bodies and wings, and a feeding tube on the front of the head, called a proboscis, coiled up when not in use. Their wings may be large, brightly coloured and patterned. Butterflies are found in most parts of the world and different species are adapted to the environments in which they live.

Like all insects, the butterfly's body is divided into three parts: head, thorax and abdomen. On the head are a pair of antennae, used for smelling, and two large compound eyes. Three pairs of legs and two pairs of wings – fore and hind – grow from the thorax. The wings are made of a very thin membrane, stretched over a framework of 'veins', in the same way as the skin of an umbrella is stretched over the frame. Tiny overlapping scales on the membrane give the wings their pattern and colour.

Male butterflies tend to be more brightly coloured than the females but the females are larger. They also have bigger wings, enabling them to fly even when they are carrying a heavy burden of eggs. A female butterfly may lay up to 3,000 eggs, always choosing the appropriate plant for the caterpillars to feed on. However, usually only one or two eggs out of a hundred hatch out and many others die as they grow through the stages of larva (caterpillar) and chrysalis (pupa) to become an imago (adult butterfly).

The imago usually has a lifespan of only a few weeks. It feeds on nectar from flowers or other sweet food, such as over-ripe fruit, which it sucks up through the proboscis. This food provides energy to fly and reproduce, but most butterflies do not need any body-building foods to see them through their short lives. In fact, a few species have mouthparts that do not open so they cannot feed.

Audience
Unknown audience – people who for some reason want to find out about butterflies. Extent of readers' prior knowledge is

Purpose
A general piece of writing describing the main characteristics of all butterflies.

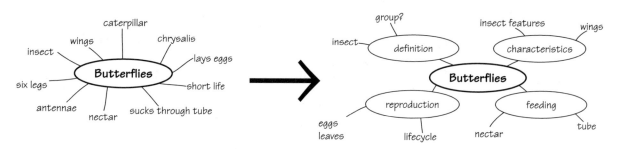

1. Brainstorm

2. Organise into categories

Organisation and content

Title: Straightforward title describing the content.

Introduction
Paragraph 1: definition
what are they? (insects: subset – *Lepidoptera*)
how is this group defined? (scales; coiled proboscis)
how wide is the group? (worldwide, adapted as necessary).

Description organised by categories
Paragraph 2: characteristics
   1. general characteristics shared with all insects
   2. focus on wings – main characteristic associated with butterflies.

Paragraph 3: reproduction
   1. male/female differences
   2. reproduction and life cycle.

Paragraph 4: feeding
   1. what/how do they eat?
   2. short lifespan – little food.

Conclusion
Paragraph 3 has dealt with life cycle, and paragraph 4 with the imago's short lifespan – this seems an appropriate place to end.

Butterflies

Butterflies belong to the order of insects known as Lepidoptera. This means they have scaly bodies and wings, and a feeding tube on the front of the head, called a proboscis, coiled up when not in use. Their wings may be large, brightly coloured and patterned. Butterflies are found in most parts of the world and different species are adapted to the environments in which they live.

Like all insects, the butterfly's body is divided into three parts: head, thorax and abdomen. On the head are a pair of antennae, used for smelling, and two large compound eyes. Three pairs of legs and two pairs of wings – fore and hind – grow from the thorax. The wings are made of a very thin membrane, stretched over a framework of 'veins', in the same way as the skin of an umbrella is stretched over the frame. Tiny overlapping scales on the membrane give the wings their pattern and colour.

Male butterflies tend to be more brightly coloured than the females but the females are larger. They also have bigger wings, enabling them to fly even when they are carrying a heavy burden of eggs. A female butterfly may lay up to 3,000 eggs, always choosing the appropriate plant for the caterpillars to feed on. However, usually only one or two eggs out of a hundred hatch out and many others die as they grow through the stages of larva (caterpillar) and chrysalis (pupa) to become an imago (adult butterfly).

The imago usually has a lifespan of only a few weeks. It feeds on nectar from flowers or other sweet food, such as over-ripe fruit, which it sucks up through the proboscis. This food provides energy to fly and reproduce, but most butterflies do not need any body-building foods to see them through their short lives. In fact, a few species have mouthparts that do not open so they cannot feed.

How to teach writing across the curriculum at key stage 2 © Sue Palmer   29

Form and style

- third-person report text – a textbook extract
- non-chronological text, organised according to categories of information

- factual writing, covering all important information and a few points of interest
- general writing about all butterflies, rather than specific facts about a particular species.

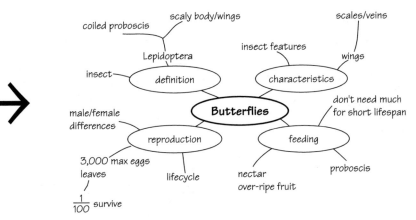

3. **Spidergram** (adding to information from 2 through further reading)

Language features

Generalised language

- Written in the **present tense** (the information is general and ongoing).
- **Generalised participants**, sometimes referred to in the plural (*insects, butterflies*) and sometimes in the 'generalised singular' (*the butterfly's body, A female butterfly, The imago*) where one butterfly is described as if it were a specimen representing the whole group.
- Use of **'weasel words' and phrases** like *tend to be, may be, usually, most*. Terms like this provide a useful 'get-out clause' for the writer when describing a wide-ranging group (it's general information with exceptions).
- Use of phrases which indicate how general/specific a particular piece of information is (*Like all insects…, a few species…*).

Formal, impersonal language

Textbooks and encyclopedias should sound clear and authoritative.

- Written in the **third person**, so we have no idea who the author is.
- Occasional use of the **passive voice** (*insects known as…; Butterflies are found…; the butterfly's body is divided into three parts*) which is formal and impersonal. However, the use of the passive is limited because the author is also trying to be clear and simple.

- Use of **technical terminology** (*Lepidoptera, proboscis*, etc.) As there is no glossary, the author sometimes tries to clarify the meanings of words which may be unfamiliar, and sometimes gambles on the reader knowing the term (*thorax, abdomen, antennae*).

Descriptive language

Descriptive language in report text differs from that in stories, poems, or even lively recount writing, in that it is concerned only with clarity, not vividness or achieving an emotional response from the reader.

- Many factual **adjectives** (e.g. *scaly bodies…wings may be large, brightly coloured and patterned; tiny, overlapping scales*) concerned with significant detail, often colour, position or size.
- Similarly, extra phrases and clauses often clarify physical features (e.g. *a feeding tube **on the front of the head**, called a proboscis, **coiled up when not in use***).
- Use of **comparison** (*in the same way as the skin of an umbrella…*), not for effect like a literary simile, but to clarify and aid understanding.
- Where possible, **quantities** and/or **dimensions** are stated (e.g. *up to 3,000 eggs*), but in highly generalised report text this is often not possible, since individual specimens vary so much.

Formatted and comparative reports

Purpose: to describe what something is like, in a way that draws comparisons or helps the reader see what things have in common.

Example: a page from a formatted encyclopedia of minibeasts.

Text structure

- classification of the particular item
- information organised in a non-chronological format, allowing comparison between different items
- description organised according to categories of information
- basic skeleton framework – a **grid**.

Language features

- present tense, third person writing
- general nouns/pronouns (not specific people/things)
- factual writing, often involving technical words and phrases
- reduced space may mean writing in note form (key words only).

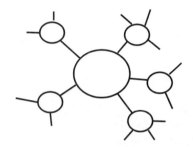
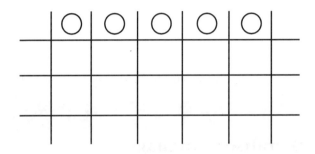

Key teaching points

- Formatted report text deals with subject matter that can be compared and contrasted, e.g. 'British birds'. The 'spider-leg' categories of a non-comparative report become the headings along one axis of the grid, e.g. *classification, habitat, feeding habits*. The headings on the other axis are the items to be compared, e.g. *sparrow, chaffinch, swallow.*

- While it seems more complex than a non-comparative report, formatted report text is actually easier to teach. By demonstrating how to write up one of the items you create a template for pupils to write about others.

- Another type of report text which is best planned on a grid is comparative writing (e.g. 'Frogs and toads', 'Christmas now and in Victorian times', 'Butterflies and moths' – see page 38), where descriptions of two items are interwoven, with attention to similarities and differences. The organisation of these texts has much in common with discussion text (see pages 64–9), and is challenging for primary children.

Common forms of formatted or comparative reports

- information leaflet
- school-project file
- tourist guidebook
- catalogue
- magazine article
- non-fiction book (e.g. geography)
- encyclopedia entry.

Big book examples of formatted or comparative report text

The Planets Heinemann Library
Festivals Round the Year Heinemann Library
Toads and their Young Longman Book Project
Investigating Fungi Rigby Magic Bean
Amazing Landforms Rigby Magic Bean
Encyclopaedia of British Wild Animals Longman Book Project
See also 'Recommended books for teachers' on pages 79–80.

BUTTERFLY   Scientific name: *Lepidoptera*

Butterflies are insects with two pairs of brightly coloured, patterned wings. Their bodies and wings are covered in tiny scales – it is the scales that give the wings their pattern. They feed through a tube on the head called a proboscis, which is coiled when not in use.

By travelling from flower to flower to suck up nectar, butterflies help with pollination. They pick up pollen on their abdomen in one flower and it brushes off on another.

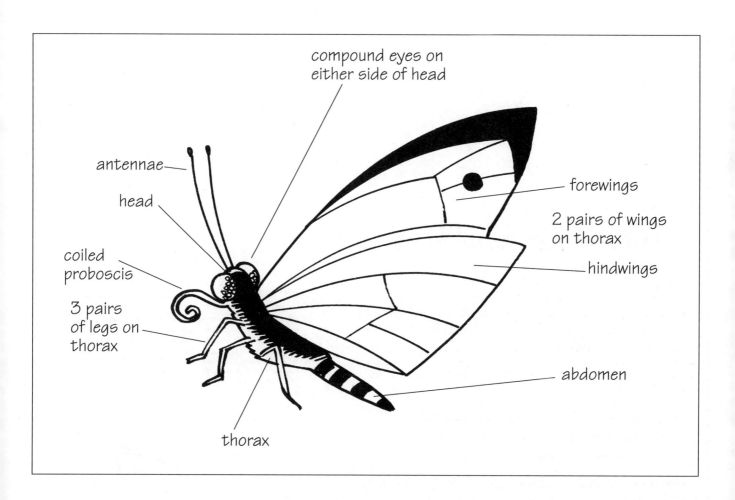

compound eyes on either side of head

antennae

head

coiled proboscis

3 pairs of legs on thorax

thorax

forewings

2 pairs of wings on thorax

hindwings

abdomen

Habitat	Feeding habits	Life cycle	Predators
Meadows, woodland, gardens	Herbivorous: nectar from flowers; ripe fruit	100s of eggs → caterpillars → pupa → adult (imago)	Birds, bats spiders, lizards, etc.

Audience
Known audience – members of the same class or school, involved in minibeasts project.

Purpose
1. to create a class encyclopedia about the minibeasts found around the school
2. to report information about each creature, based on a research format.

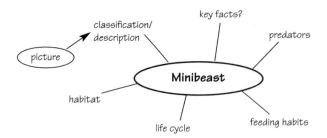

picture → classification/ description

key facts?

predators

Minibeast

habitat

life cycle

feeding habits

	Classfication	Key facts	Habitat	Feeding habits	Life cycle	Predators
Butterfly	Insect Lepidoptera	1. scales and coiled proboscis 2. helps pollination	Meadows woodlands gardens	Herbivorous – nectar ripe fruit	100s of eggs → caterpillars → pupa → imago	Birds, bats, spiders, frogs, lizards, small mammals
Worm						
Woodlouse						

Organisation and content

Organisation determined by format – layout very important.

Heading: name of minibeast, in large capital letters to be seen easily by the reader (this also aids alphabetical organisation of encyclopedia). Scientific name in italics.

Main text: sentences summing up main facts about butterflies –

1. what distinguishes them from other insects
2. their importance in plant reproduction.

Written in coherent sentences.

Picture: simplified diagram with labels. Leader lines drawn with ruler (as often as possible leader lines are horizontal). Labels – key words only (print writing style used to differentiate from text).

Boxed text: notes summing up remaining key facts about butterflies – key words only; punctuation, arrows, and layout used to clarify meaning.

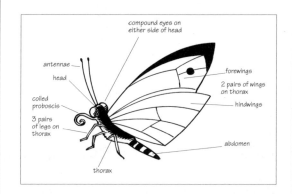

BUTTERFLY   Scientific name: *Lepidoptera*

Butterflies are insects with two pairs of brightly coloured, patterned wings. Their bodies and wings are covered in tiny scales – it is the scales that give the wings their pattern. They feed through a tube on the head called a proboscis, which is coiled when not in use.
   By travelling from flower to flower to suck up nectar, butterflies help with pollination. They pick up pollen on their abdomen in one flower and it brushes off on another.

Habitat	Feeding habits	Life cycle	Predators
Meadows, woodland, gardens	Herbivorous: nectar from flowers; ripe fruit	100s of eggs → caterpillars → pupa → adult (imago)	Birds, bats spiders, lizards, etc.

→

Form and style

- report text written to a format
- non-chronological text, organised according to agreed categories of information

- key facts only, no superfluous detail, but must be clear to readers other than the author – some coherent sentences, some information in note form.

Language features

Generalised report language

- The information refers to all British butterflies, so the language is highly generalised: **present tense, plural referents** (*butterflies, insects*).
- Language is formal and impersonal: **third person**, so we have no idea who the author is; use of **technical terminology** (*Lepidoptera, proboscis, herbivorous,* etc.). In an encyclopedia of this type, where there is little room for further explanation, one would expect a glossary to clarify unusual technical terms.

Descriptive language

Report text calls for objective, observational description, not vivid, emotional language.

- Factual **adjectives** (e.g. *brightly coloured, patterned wings; tiny scales*), concerned with significant detail – colour, position or size.

Description of distinguishing features (*…which is coiled when not in use*).

Features of notes

The format is designed to include the maximum information in the minimum space. Labels on the picture and boxed information are therefore in note form. However, these notes must be intelligible to the general reader.

- **Key words**, notably **nouns** and **verbs** (essential adjectives only: *compound eyes, coiled proboscis, ripe fruit*). **Determiners** (including the words *the* and *a*) not used at all.
- Use of **abbreviations** and **symbols** for brevity (*etc.* and →). Use of figures rather than words (*3 pairs; 100s of eggs*).
- Use of **punctuation** to clarify meaning in abbreviated text (comma, colon, semicolon).

Year 3 report writing

NLS text-level references

T1 reading: 17, 18, 21, non-fiction text structures and key facts

T1 writing: 22, record information from texts read; write simple non-chronological reports for known audience.

NLS sentence-level links

T1:   verbs and tense; presentational devices; writing in sentences

T2:   notes, deleting words.

Content and organisation

Make a formatted class book based on our encyclopedia of minibeasts or another topic of interest (e.g. an encyclopedia of British mammals or of transport). Create a format for the page, with agreed headings, as in the example on page 33. Write one page of your book in shared writing by:

- using the page format (or a grid, as in our example on page 34) to write rough notes on your chosen topic
- showing how to draw and label a simplified diagram
- using the notes to make a neat final page (some sentences, some notes in boxes).

Ask pupils to use the same page format to research, write notes, draft a diagram, then write up their own pages for the book, based on your model.

Language features

- Writing in sentences: demonstrate how to convert the notes in our example text (see page 33) into sentences, e.g. *Butterflies are generally found in meadows, woodlands and gardens.* Discuss the differences between notes and sentences.
- Writing notes, word deletion: demonstrate how to turn sentences into notes, e.g. *insects – 2 pairs wings; scales on body/wings; proboscis (can coil).*
- Verbs and tense: demonstrate how to use present tense for non-chronological factual writing about general topics, as above. Contrast with recounts (see page 24). Always use present tense on spidergram notes.
- Presentational devices show how:
  - the use of headings and subheadings links to the categorisation in a spidergram
  - writing style can help differentiate parts of the text: capitals for headings, print for labels, joined writing for main text.

Using spidergrams for non-chronological note-taking

- Ensure children recognise the difference between information that can be organised chronologically and that which can't. In all areas of the curriculum, use spidergrams yourself to illustrate/record the main points of subjects which do not have a chronological basis.

- Encourage children to use this technique to organise their thoughts when planning (e.g. when developing a character or a setting for story-writing).

- Use when teaching about key words for note-taking – on a spidergram there isn't room for irrelevance – just enough words to act as an aide memoire.

Year 4 report writing

NLS text-level references

T1 reading: 16, 17, layout and presentation
T1 writing: 27, write a non-chronological report using organisational devices
T2 writing: 21, make short notes.

NLS sentence-level links

T1: verbs and tense; adverbs of manner
T2: adjectives and adjectival phrases.

Content and organisation

Demonstrate the links between spidergram notes and organisational devices.

- In reading, investigate how report text is split up into sections (with headings) and subsections (with subheadings). Convert the content into spidergram notes: overall title in the centre; headings on the spider legs; subheadings radiating from there. Perhaps add key words. Ask children to do the same with other report text material.
- For writing, choose suitable familiar content from any curriculum area to arrange on a spidergram and use as skeleton notes. Discuss organisation, using the spidergram to dictate sections (with headings) and subsections (with subheadings).

Language features

- Verbs and tense: continue to emphasise the use of the present tense, except in historical reports (e.g. the Greeks or Victorian clothes) which describe conditions no longer extant.
- Adjectives, adjectival phrases and adverbs of manner: in reading, investigate how these are used in:
  - fiction and poetry (and sometimes recount text): for vividness and effect, to engage and excite the reader
  - non-chronological reports (and most other non-fiction text): to give necessary, factual detail (see notes on pages 31 and 35). In writing non-chronological reports, encourage the use of descriptive words and phrases to give necessary factual detail; demonstrate how to avoid flowery or value-laden description.

How to BOS

The stages in making a spidergram can be summarised by the acronym BOS.

- **B**rainstorm what you know about the subject. Depending on how familiar you are with the topic, you can do this orally, mentally or jot words and phrases down on paper, in any order. If it's a subject you know nothing at all about, you might start with some research, seeking out key words.

- **O**rganise the material into categories. Think how your facts could be clustered together under headings. Come up with four to six main categories, which could then, if necessary, break down into subcategories. More research may help you choose categories.

- **S**pidergram it. Write the topic title in the middle and the names of the categories at the end of the spider legs. Then subcategorise if necessary, or just write relevant key words. Further research will yield more information to note in appropriate places (see example on page 30).

Year 5 report writing

NLS text-level references

T1 writing: 26, make notes for different purposes, e.g. cues for a talk

T2 writing: 22, plan, compose, edit, refine short non-chronological texts.

NLS sentence-level links

T1: writing for different audiences and purposes.

Content and organisation

Notes for a talk: ask pupils to create their own spidergram notes to use both as the basis of writing and as a prompt for a prepared talk.

Language features

- Audience and purpose: investigate features of formal, impersonal style and the use of 'weasel words' for generalised accounts (see notes on page 31).
- Audience and purpose: contrast the two example texts, discussing how audience and purpose affect layout, writing style, vocabulary.

Paragraphing in reports

- In reading reports, note how the author has decided on paragraph breaks, e.g. in the example text on page 29, ask pupils to summarise the content of each paragraph.

- Relate to the organisation of notes on a spidergram. Paragraphs are the final stage in the hierarchy: title, sections, subsections, paragraphs.

- In a short report text, as on page 29, there is no room for headings and subheadings.

- Give pupils opportunities to research and create spidergram notes for a similar short piece. Discuss how the spidergram will determine paragraphs.

Comparative report writing

Another common type of text is the comparative report: text which compares and contrasts two or more items. Like formatted text, this is based on a grid skeleton, but it is then written as coherent text, interweaving the items in the same way as discussion text interweaves points. Enlarge the text below and use to investigate language features of comparative text.

Butterflies and moths are two families of creature within the order of insects known as *Lepidoptera* (from the Greek words for 'scaly wings'). This means they have **a great deal in common**: they **both** have scales all over their bodies and wings, giving the wings their characteristic colours and patterns; they **both also** have a proboscis – the feeding tube on the front of their head – which can be coiled up when not in use.

There are **a number of observable differences** between butterflies and moths. **For instance, most butterflies** fly by day, **while most moths** fly by night. **Butterflies are, on the whole,** more brightly coloured **whereas moths are more likely** to be shades of brown and grey. **Most butterflies** hold their wings upright over their backs, **while moths tend** to rest with their wings folded flat. **Finally,** butterflies have antennae which are knobbed at the tip; moths' antennae are either feathered or plain.

There are, however, about ten thousand species of butterfly in the world, and even more species of moths. Each species is adapted to its habitat, so the variety within both families is enormous. The distinction between the two is an artificial one, decided upon by scientists, and there is no one single feature that separates all butterflies from all moths. **On the whole, the similarities between the two families far outweigh the differences.**

Year 6 report writing

NLS text-level references

T1 reading: features of report text
T1 writing: 16, journalistic style;
             17, write non-chronological reports
T3 reading: 19, review a range of text types
T3 writing: 22, select appropriate style and form
             for purpose and audience.

NLS sentence-level links

T1: active and passive.

Content and organisation

Ask pupils to research and plan a non-fiction leaflet on a topic of interest.

- Use BOS and research skills to create notes on a spidergram.
- Design layout, including headings, subheadings, illustrations, etc.
- Draft each section of the leaflet, using appropriate style.
- 'Publish' leaflet, either in neat handwriting or using word processor.

Language features

- Features of report text: use the examples and notes on pages 30–31 and 34–5 to revise the main language features, including generalised language, factual description, impersonal language and present tense.
- Active and passive: find instances of the passive voice in the first example text (see page 31). Establish that it is used to maintain an impersonal voice (try transforming into the active, e.g. *We call this order Lepidoptera..., You can find butterflies in most parts of the world*). Discuss why an impersonal voice is appropriate in this context.

Report checklist

Organisation

- Does the introductory paragraph orientate the reader, so that he or she has a rough idea of what the piece will be about? ❏
- Is the text organised into sections or paragraphs, so that the underlying structure (the way information has been categorised) is clear? ❏
- Is this supported by the layout – headings, subheadings, paragraph breaks? ❏
- Do the closing statements bring the text to a satisfactory conclusion? ❏

Language features

- Is the text consistently in the present tense (except for historical reports)? ❏
- Is the text written in an appropriately formal, impersonal style (for instance, with occasional use of the passive)? ❏
- Is the style appropriately general? ❏
- If technical vocabulary is used, is its meaning always made clear (as appropriate to the text's audience)? ❏
- Is descriptive language used factually, to describe and clarify, rather than for vividness and effect? ❏
- Are all statements based on fact, rather than value judgement? ❏

Unit 3 – Instruction text

Purpose: to tell someone how to do or make something.

Example: instructions for a craft activity.

Text structure

- title or opening sets out what's to be achieved
- starts with a list of items required
- often accompanied by diagram(s)
- sequenced steps in order to achieve the goal – what to do, in time order
- skeleton framework – a **flowchart** ('you do this, then you do this, etc.').

Language features

- usually written in the imperative, present tense (some instructions require third person narrative – see below)
- in time order (often numbered steps and/or time connectives)
- clear, concise language, e.g. adjectives and adverbs chosen for clarity rather than vividness and effect
- the author addresses an anonymous reader, not a named individual.

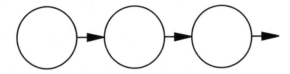

Key teaching points

- Simple instruction text is very direct, and thus fairly easy for young children to write. It is a useful vehicle for demonstrating major differences between the use of language in fiction and factual writing (e.g. descriptive language chosen for clarity, not vividness).

- Simple instruction text speaks directly to the reader, using imperative verbs (e.g. *Do this, do that*), but occasionally instructions may be written in the third person. When more than one person is involved (e.g. in a game), clarity requires that they be named (e.g. *player A*, *the batting team*) and their actions described impersonally.

- It is very helpful if children can actually carry out the process concerned before they write. For this reason, cross-curricular links to art, DT, IT, PE, and so on are invaluable.

- Diagrams help make instructions clear. Children also need to be taught how to draw simple, clear diagrams and label them appropriately.

Common forms of instruction text

- recipe
- technical manual (e.g. for car, computer)
- non-fiction book (e.g. sports skills, art)
- timetable, route finder
- list of rules
- posters, notices, signs
- sewing or knitting pattern
- instructions on packaging (e.g. cooking or washing instructions).

Big book examples of instruction text

Round the World Cookbook Longman

Making Puppets Rigby Magic Bean

Broomsticks and Balloons Heinemann Literacy World Stage 3 NF Big Book A

Making Party Decorations OUP Literacy Web

See also 'Recommended books for teachers' on pages 79–80.

How to make a papier mâché bowl

You need:

half a cup of flour

half a cup of water

a tablespoon of salt

a container for mixing paste

newspaper, torn into thin strips

a balloon, blown up and knotted

a strip of card (about 30 cm by 4 cm)

sticky tape and scissors

paint and brushes

varnish and brush.

Papier mâché is the French for 'chewed paper'! It is a mixture of paper and paste that hardens when dry.

1. First make the paste. Put the flour and salt into the container and gradually mix in the water until it is thick and creamy.

2. Dip the strips of newspaper into the paste and smooth them down on to the unknotted end of the balloon. Cover enough of the balloon to make a bowl shape. Use three or four layers of paper strips. Leave to dry.

3. Make a base for the bowl by taping the card into a circle shape, and taping it on to the balloon. Cover with a few more pasted strips to hold it in place.

4. Pop the balloon and remove its plastic skin. Ask a grown-up to help you trim the top of the bowl, and smooth more pasted strips over the edges to finish it off. Leave to dry.

5. Paint the bowl in bright colours. When it is dry, brush on a final coat of varnish.

Audience
Readers (probably children) who want to know how to make a papier mâché bowl.

Purpose
- to help the reader achieve this aim easily and safely
- to explain how to make papier mâché, how to use a balloon as a mould, how to finish the bowl.

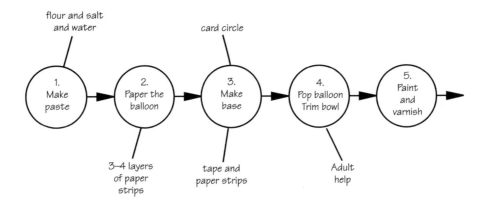

flour and salt and water

card circle

1. Make paste → 2. Paper the balloon → 3. Make base → 4. Pop balloon Trim bowl → 5. Paint and varnish →

3–4 layers of paper strips

tape and paper strips

Adult help

Organisation and content

Title: a statement of what is to be achieved.
This is reinforced and clarified by the illustration at the foot of the page.

List of equipment
- provided first, so that the reader can ensure that everything is available before starting the process
- items listed vertically (and in order of use) for easy reading and checking.

Boxed information
Extra information (explaining a term likely to be unfamiliar to readers) is held separate from the rest of the text, so that it does not interfere with the clarity of the instructions.

Sequenced instructions
Numbered steps aid clarity. These act like paragraphs in other texts: the visual/spatial arrangement helps the reader break up the information into manageable chunks. Each numbered step sums up an important stage in the process (as shown in the flowchart above):

    1. making the paste
    2. papering the balloon
    3. making a base
    4. finishing the bowl
    5. painting and varnishing.

Illustration
Illustration of the final product helps the reader understand exactly what is to be achieved. Further diagrams throughout the text would also aid comprehension, but were omitted for teaching purposes.

How to make a papier mâché bowl

You need:
  half a cup of flour
  half a cup of water
  a tablespoon of salt
  a container for mixing paste
  newspaper, torn into thin strips
  a balloon, blown up and knotted
  a strip of card (about 30 cm by 4 cm)
  sticky tape and scissors
  paint and brushes
  varnish and brush.

Papier mâché is the French for 'chewed paper'! It is a mixture of paper and paste that hardens when dry.

1. First make the paste. Put the flour and salt into the container and gradually mix in the water until it is thick and creamy.
2. Dip the strips of newspaper into the paste and smooth them down on to the unknotted end of the balloon. Cover enough of the balloon to make a bowl shape. Use three or four layers of paper strips. Leave to dry.
3. Make a base for the bowl by taping the card into a circle shape, and taping it on to the balloon. Cover with a few more pasted strips to hold it in place.
4. Pop the balloon and remove its plastic skin. Ask a grown-up to help you trim the top of the bowl, and smooth more pasted strips over the edges to finish it off. Leave to dry.
5. Paint the bowl in bright colours. When it is dry, brush on a final coat of varnish.

→

Form and style

- instruction text – clear, simple, speaking directly to the reader; no unnecessary detail
- outcome, equipment required, and all steps in the process must be included
- layout must illustrate sequence – would diagrams help?

Language features

Addressing the reader

- Written in the **imperative present tense**, to speak directly to the reader as he or she carries out the instructions.
- The imperative is always in the **second person** (e.g. *you* in step 4), which applies generally to all readers. All references to people are generalised rather than specific (e.g. *a grown-up* in step 4)*.
- There are many short simple sentences (*First make the paste*) and compound sentences where two ideas are simply linked by *and*. This mirrors the simple language patterns of speech, as though the writer were talking directly to the reader.

Clarity and relevance

Instructions must be totally clear.

- In the list of equipment, **quantities** and/or **dimensions** are stated explicitly where necessary.
- **Necessary detail** is provided but no superfluous detail (e.g. the list specifies that the balloon is *blown up and knotted* but doesn't mention the colour of the balloon, which is irrelevant).
- Use of the **imperative** means that the verb is usually at the beginning of the sentence, which gives it prominence. The verbs are chosen for maximum clarity, not for descriptive effect (e.g. *make, mix, dip*).
- **Adverbs** and **adjectives** are included for clarity and precision, not for effect (e.g. **gradually** *mix in the water until it is* **thick** *and* **creamy**). All these descriptive words are necessary to the reader's understanding of the instructions. There is no value-laden description (e.g. *lovely and thick*) or vivid, descriptive language (e.g. *languorously, viscous*).
- **Simple language patterns** (mainly simple and compound sentences, see above).

Sequence

- **Numbers** clearly indicate the sequence of the steps (see 'Sequenced instructions' opposite).
- These are backed up occasionally by **sequential connectives** (*First, when...*).

Awareness of audience

The readers of these instructions are likely to be children. Simplicity and clarity (see above) are therefore doubly important.

- There is also an assumption that the reader will need help with areas which could be a safety issue (*Ask a grown-up to help you trim...*).

---

* When instructions are given in the third person (see second key teaching point on page 40), these are generalised human agents – e.g. *player A, the batting team* – rather than specific participants.

Year 3 instruction writing

NLS text-level references

T2 reading: 12, 13, 14, 15, identify purposes of instructional texts; compare and evaluate examples; note organisation; use

T2 writing: 16, write sequenced instructions, using organisational devices and writing frames.

NLS sentence-level links

T1: range of presentational devices
T1: verb tenses
T2: use of adjectives, second person verbs.

Content and organisation

Focus on presentational devices.

- See 'Numbers, lists, pictures, boxes' below.
- Investigate pictures and diagrams in instruction text, and help children recognise the need for simplicity and clear labelling. Give opportunities for drawing and evaluating diagrams.

Language features

- Use of adjectives: compare the adjectives used in instructions (e.g. our example) to those in fiction and poetry; help children recognise the different way language is used depending on purpose and audience.
- Second person verbs: provide a list of verbs (e.g. *to eat, to sing, to smile, to throw*) and ask pupils to use them in an instruction (e.g. *Eat your dinner*). Discuss who is being addressed on each occasion (i.e. the second person, *you*). Talk about first, second, third person and make a list of sentences for each verb, e.g. *I eat my dinner; Eat your dinner; he eats his dinner*.

Numbers, lists, pictures, boxes

- Provide pupils with a range of instruction texts, preferably genuine published material:
  - books of recipes, craft ideas, science activities
  - magazine cuttings of DIY ideas, recipes
  - rules, e.g. for school, games, membership of clubs
  - instructions for using household equipment, as printed on packaging and labels, or in manuals
  - signs and notices, e.g. *Keep off the grass, Keep Out, Take your litter home with you*
  - travel instructions, e.g. timetables, route finders, map books.

- Discuss the range of organisational and presentational devices (e.g. *Why do you think they've put this bit in a box? What's the point of using capitals here? Why is there such a lot of space around this bit?*). Help children see that clarity and simplicity are crucial to instructions.

- Ask children in pairs to copy, photocopy or (if it's expendable material) cut out at least one good example of a presentational device, and make it into a mini-poster, with a caption explaining what it is (including the correct terminology) and why it is helpful in instruction text.

- Each pair can then explain their findings to the rest of the class, and their mini-posters can be compiled into a collage.

Year 4 instruction writing

NLS text-level references

T1 reading: 22, identify key features of instructions including sequence and imperative mood

T1 writing: 25, write clear instructions; 26, improve coherence through link phrases and organisational devices

T2 writing: 21, 23 note-taking and diagrammatic representation.

NLS sentence-level links

T1: verbs, person, and tense; adverbs

T2, T3: connectives and linking words

T3: grammatical changes, e.g questions to commands.

Content and organisation

- Help children recognise that conventional instructions consist of four elements: title, list, diagram(s), and staged steps. In shared reading, help them see how the staged steps can be converted into a simple flowchart containing key words (as in our example on page 42).

- When they are learning a new skill – in art, PE, IT, etc. – encourage children to create a simple flowchart of the stages, with each stage in a 'bubble'. If you keep the bubbles small, it will encourage them to keep key words down to a minimum. The flowchart can act as an aide-memoire but also, if necessary, as content for instruction writing.

Language features

- Adverbs: as with adjectives (see Year 3) note the different ways adverbs are used in instructions and fiction/poetry.

- Verbs: person, imperative mood. With pupils create a selection of second person statements (e.g. *You can sing*), questions (e.g. *Can you sing?*), commands (e.g. *Sing!*). Display them on labelled posters, and add the word *imperative* to the third: Commands (*imperative*). Explain the connection between this word and *emperor, imperial, imperious*. Discuss the differences between the three types of sentence in terms of their meaning, grammar, word order and punctuation. Note that not all statements or questions can be converted into the imperative. Find examples of each kind of sentence in shared texts – note the preponderance of imperatives in instruction writing.

First, next, then, finally

Video part of a TV cookery programme and count the number of times the presenter says *and then* or just *then* while demonstrating a recipe. Establish that the presenter uses this simple connective to show s/he is moving from one step in the process to another. Connectives are like signposts to the audience: 'I've finished that bit...now we're on to something else.'

And then is a common connective in speech, when we are in the same place as our audience and they can actually see what we are doing. In written language, the repeated use of *and then* is boring to read, and actually makes the text less, rather than more, clear. Collect alternative ways of signalling the move between steps from recipe and craft books, including numbering, bullet points, sequential connectives, para-graphing and layout.

Ask pupils to return to some instruction text they made earlier, and improve the coherence by better use of these connective devices.

Year 5 instruction writing

NLS text-level references

T1 reading: 22, evaluate instruction texts in terms of purpose, organisation, layout, usefulness

T1 writing: 25, write and test instruction texts.

NLS sentence-level links

T1: proofread and edit for clarity; verbs – tense, imperative, person, transformations.

Content and organisation

Plan it, make it, write it, test it

- In Design and Technology, ask pupils to design and make an artefact of some kind (e.g. a musical instrument, based on knowledge acquired in Science on sound). They should think through the design stages carefully in advance, and create a simple flowchart of the steps they intend to follow (see Year 4). They could also create a diagram of the finished artefact, as they intend it to look.

- As they carry out the activity, the flowchart/diagram may be changed and annotated, as plans and outcomes change. This provides a working record of the activity, which can eventually be kept in their DT folder.

- The flowchart can also be used as skeleton notes for writing instructions. Pupils' experience of making the artefact means they have expert knowledge of the content of the instructions. In shared reading, concentrate on organisational and linguistic features of instruction text.

- Bearing this in mind, pupils should write up instructions for making their artefacts, proofreading and editing them for clarity. The instructions can be placed in a hat, and during the next DT lesson each child should draw out a set of instructions to read and follow. Readers can then feed back to writers.

Language features

- Verbs – tense, imperative, person, transformations:
  - Make an enlarged copy of the text in the box (our example text converted into a recount). Read with the children and ask which would be easier to follow if you wanted to make a bowl: recount or instructions? Discuss why. Then discuss differences in tense and person between the two texts.
  - Establish that one of the main effects of the imperative is to emphasise the verbs (which are critical in instructions) by bringing them up front.
  - Ask pupils to convert sections of instruction text to recount and vice versa.

Our papier mâché bowl

First we made the paste. We put the flour and salt into the container and gradually mixed in the water until it was thick and creamy. Then we dipped the strips of newspaper into the paste and smoothed them down on to the unknotted end of the balloon. We covered enough of the balloon to make a bowl shape, using three or four layers of paper strips. Then we left it to dry.

We made a base for the bowl by taping the card into a circle shape and taping it on to the balloon. We covered it with a few more pasted strips to hold it in place. Next we popped the balloon and removed its plastic skin. Mrs Bruce helped us trim the top of the bowl, and we smoothed more pasted strips over the edges to finish it off, then left it to dry.

Finally, we painted the bowl in bright colours. When it was dry, we brushed on a final coat of varnish.

Year 6 instruction writing

NLS text-level references

T3 reading: 19, review a range of text types
T3 writing: 22, select appropriate style and form
for purpose and audience.

NLS sentence-level links

T3: language conventions of instructions.

Content and organisation

- Revise the four-part nature of instruction text: informative title, list of what's required, staged instructions (which can be represented as a simple flowchart), diagram(s).
- Revise the organisational and presentational devices that can be used, including numbering, layout, headings, bullets.

Language features

- Use checklist below to revise major languge features.

Instruction checklist

Organisation

- Does the title (or opening) set out what's to be achieved? ❏
- If equipment or ingredients are required, are these given in a clear list? ❏
- Is there a series of sequenced steps to achieve the goal? ❏
- Does the layout and presentation make the sequence clear and easy to follow? ❏
- If appropriate, is there a clearly labelled diagram (or diagrams)? ❏
- Are other organisational devices used for clarity, e.g. boxes for extra information, bullet points, numbers? ❏

Language features

- Is the text consistently in the imperative present tense (except when there is more than one person/team involved)? ❏
- If more than one person/team is involved, are they named or labelled in some way so they are clearly distinguishable? ❏
- Is the language and vocabulary clear and concise? ❏
- Are quantities and measurements clearly stated wherever necessary? ❏
- Is descriptive language used for clarity rather than vividness or effect? ❏
- Are time connectives or other devices used to ensure that the sequence of the stages is clear? ❏

Unit 4 – Explanation text

Purpose: to explain how or why something happens.

Example: an extract from a science textbook.

Text structure

- title often asks a question or defines the process to be explained
- text usually opens with general statement(s) to introduce the topic
- a series of logical steps explaining the process, usually in time order
- often accompanied by diagram(s)
- basic skeleton framework – a **flowchart** ('this happens, leading to this, which leads to this').

Language features

- present tense (the process is general)
- time connectives and other devices to aid chronological structure
- causal connectives and other devices demonstrating cause and effect.

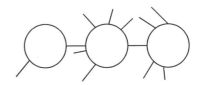

Key teaching points

- Explanations are difficult to write. Before putting pen to paper, children must thoroughly understand the process they are about to explain. Making a skeleton framework first – especially a flowchart and/or labelled diagram – develops understanding.

- However, even making the flowchart can be tricky! There are many possible variations, depending upon the process in question, for example:

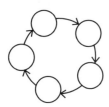

a **cycle**

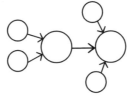

multiple causes and/or effects

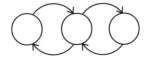

reversible effects

- Pupils need to see plenty of models created by the teacher. They also need time to experiment with different ways of representing a process (collaborative work is particularly useful). However, the process of developing a suitable skeleton framework can in itself aid understanding.

- When children come to write, encourage them to include flowcharts or diagrams alongside their text. Most explanation is enhanced by visual representation (e.g. the example text opposite would be easier to understand if a flowchart were provided alongside, but this was omitted for teaching purposes).

Common forms of explanation text

- textbook
- encyclopedia entry
- non-fiction book (e.g. geography, biology)
- technical manual (e.g. for car, dishwasher)
- question-and-answer articles and leaflets
- write-up of science experiment.

Big book examples of explanation text

World Weather Longman Book Project
The Body BBC (Find Out About)
Broomsticks and Balloons Heinemann Literacy
World Stage 3 NF Big Book A
How Cows Make Milk Rigby Magic Bean
See also 'Recommended books for teachers' on pages 79–80.

Why do people die if they stop breathing?

In order to stay alive, human beings need a constant supply of **oxygen** (a gas found in the air) to all parts of the body. They also need to rid their bodies of a waste gas called **carbon dioxide**, which would otherwise poison them.

These two gases are carried round the body in the blood. **Veins** carry blood to the heart and **arteries** carry blood away from the heart. Both veins and arteries divide into millions of tiny **capillary blood vessels**. Gases can move between the blood in the capillaries and the tiny **cells** which make up the human body.

When a human being breathes in, the air goes down into the **lungs**, which are like two spongy bags filled with millions of air sacs. Oxygen from the air passes through the sacs into the capillary blood vessels. The blood then carries the oxygen through a vein to the **heart**.

The heart pumps this oxygen-carrying blood around the whole body through arteries which divide into capillaries to reach the body cells. Oxygen passes from the blood to the cells, and carbon dioxide (the waste gas) passes from the cells into the blood. Veins take this waste-carrying blood back to the heart, which pumps it back to the lungs. There the carbon dioxide passes into the air sacs.

When the human being breathes out, the carbon dioxide is pushed back out into the air. Breathing in and out is therefore essential because it ensures that life-giving oxygen is constantly replaced and poisonous carbon dioxide expelled.

Audience

Readers who want to know the answer to the question in the title, but who know little about the subject.

Purpose

1. to provide the answer as simply and clearly as possible
2. to explain the roles of the lungs, heart, and circulation of the blood in maintaining life.

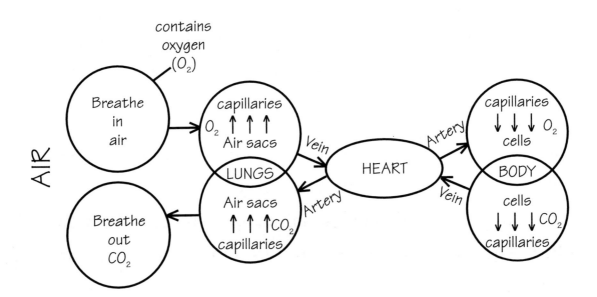

Organisation and content

Title: a question requiring an explanation of a process.

Introduction

Paragraph 1: general statement of why we breathe

   1. one sentence about oxygen
   2. one sentence about carbon dioxide.

Paragraph 2: defines some key terms (*veins, arteries, capillary blood vessels*) to be used in the explanation. Giving these definitions in advance means the explanation can proceed more smoothly.

Explanation

Paragraph 3: the first three stages in the process, taking oxygen from the air, through the blood to the heart (as shown in the flowchart above).

Paragraph 4: the next three stages in the process, returning the blood to the lungs (as shown in the flowchart above).

Conclusion

Final paragraph: concluding statement of why we breathe

   1. first sentence: conclusion of the process
   2. second sentence: summary of the answer to the question.

Why do people die if they stop breathing?

In order to stay alive, human beings need a constant supply of **oxygen** (a gas found in the air) to all parts of the body. They also need to rid their bodies of a waste gas called **carbon dioxide**, which would otherwise poison them.

These two gases are carried round the body in the blood. **Veins** carry blood to the heart and **arteries** carry blood away from the heart. Both veins and arteries divide into millions of tiny **capillary blood vessels**. Gases can move between the blood in the capillaries and the tiny **cells** which make up the human body.

When a human being breathes in, the air goes down into the **lungs**, which are like two spongy bags filled with millions of air sacs. Oxygen from the air passes through the sacs into the capillary blood vessels. The blood then carries the oxygen through a vein to the **heart**.

The heart pumps this oxygen-carrying blood around the whole body through arteries which divide into capillaries to reach the body cells. Oxygen passes from the blood to the cells, and carbon dioxide (the waste gas) passes from the cells into the blood. Veins take this waste-carrying blood back to the heart, which pumps it back to the lungs. There the carbon dioxide passes into the air sacs.

When the human being breathes out, the carbon dioxide is pushed back out into the air. Breathing in and out is therefore essential because it ensures that life-giving oxygen is constantly replaced and poisonous carbon dioxide expelled.

→

Form and style

- explanation text – general, impersonal, formal, but also clear and simple
- technical terminology must be explained
- layout must illustrate sequence – paragraphs; would diagrams or pictures help?

Language features

General language

- Written in the **present tense** because this is a general process, happening time and time again.
- It refers to *human beings* (a general term), not just specific named people.

Formal, impersonal language

Explanations should sound clear and authoritative, not personal and chatty. They should:

- be written in the **third person** (*human beings/they* – not we)
- occasionally use the **passive voice** (e.g. *gases are carried, oxygen is constantly replaced*) which is formal and impersonal. However, the use of the passive is limited because it can be difficult to understand (the author has tried to balance formality and clarity)
- frequently use formal, **technical terminology** (see below) rather than simplified language
- use **complex sentences** (see 'Cause and effect' below) which are a feature of formal written language.

Technical terminology

Technical terms are necessary for accuracy but must be defined for the non-technical reader. In the absence of a glossary, the author uses a number of techniques to provide information:

- brackets: *oxygen (a gas found in the air)*
- explanation given before the noun: *a waste gas called carbon dioxide*
- explanatory subordinate clause: *which would otherwise poison them*
- an entire paragraph (paragraph 2) providing definitions of words to be used later.

Sequence

Processes usually involve a sequence of events:

- **sequential connectives** (*When..., then*) help to indicate the stages in the sequence
- **paragraph breaks** indicate significant stages, but cohesion between paragraphs must be maintained (e.g. *The blood then carries the oxygen.../The heart pumps this oxygen-carrying blood...*).

Cause and effect

- **Causal connectives** (*In order to..., When..., therefore..., because...*).
- **Complex sentences** show the interrelationships between the ideas expressed in each clause.
- Clear links between the **title**, the **opening statement** and the final sentence, which is a **summary** of the explanation, providing the answer to the question.

Year 3 explanation writing

NLS text-level references

T2 writing: 17, note-making, including flowchart format.

NLS sentence-level links

T2: deleting words to see which are essential to meaning.

Content and organisation

Focus on how to make flowcharts.

- Investigate flowcharts and diagrams in published texts (see list on page 48), noting how few words authors need to use when they combine them with graphic organisers and illustrations.

- Make flowcharts to help explain processes in other curricular areas (see below).

Language features

Words and pictures

- Provide a flowchart or diagram for a familiar process without any accompanying labels or explanatory text. Discuss with pupils and ask them to help you provide labels/minimum text to make it clear to a reader.

- Discuss the sort of words you have used. (Generally, labels consist mainly of nouns and verbs.) Discuss any other symbols you have used, e.g. arrows, and what they mean.

- Now ask the pupils to explain the process in words for someone who is unable to see your diagram/flowchart. Discuss how language changes when the visual display is absent and the burden of explanation falls completely on the words.

Making flowcharts

- Whenever possible, and throughout your teaching, demonstrate how to construct flowcharts and diagrams to help you explain (and children understand) processes in all curriculum areas. Don't be afraid to change/improve on flowcharts as you go on. It's difficult to get them right first time, and children should know this.

- Use a variety of forms of flowcharts (e.g. cycles, reversible flowcharts – see examples on page 48) so children see that this type of skeleton is very flexible, and depends on the process concerned.

- Display flowcharts and diagrams in the classroom as part of cross-curricular work.

- Give children a chance to try their own. Choose a familiar process from any curricular area. Ask them, in pairs, to design a flowchart and/or diagram to represent it. Encourage children to draft and redraft if necessary, and to create final tidy versions. Discuss the success (or otherwise) of their efforts. On the basis of the most successful, create an effective shared version.

Year 4 explanation writing

NLS text-level references

T2 reading: 19, uses of paragraphing; 20, key features of explanation text (purpose, structure, language, presentation)

T2 writing: 24, 25, writing explanations using paragraphing and other conventions.

NLS sentence-level links

T2: the use of commas, connectives and full stops to join/separate clauses

T3: the use of connectives, e.g. adverbs, adverb phrases.

Content and organisation

- Continue to discuss the audience and purpose of explanation texts in shared reading (see list on page 48), and how this affects the layout, presentation, structure and organisation of the text.
- In particular, discuss the significance of:
  - accompanying illustrations and diagrams
  - headed sections, bullet-pointing, numbering of points.

  Why has the author chosen to use particular organisational features in each case?
- Choose a process familiar to pupils from another curricular area and, with the class, compile a flowchart/diagram to illustrate it. Discuss how the organisational features mentioned above might be used in writing up the explanation.

Language features

- Key features of explanation text (T20). Draw attention to these in shared reading (see example notes on page 51). Focus especially on:
  - present tense (because this is a general and frequently repeated process)
  - sequential connectives and paragraphing, indicating sequence of events
  - formal tone (third person, impersonal writing; technical terminology)
  - causal language and punctuation (see activity below).

Making causal connections

- From reading, collect a range of connectives and language constructions that indicate cause and effect, such as:
  - conjunctions (used to join clauses within a sentence), e.g. **because, so, if** (*this happens, something else follows*); **when** (*this happens, something follows*)
  - sentence connectives (used to make links between two sentences), e.g. **therefore, consequently, as a result**
  - sentence openings: **The reason...is that...; This results in...; This causes...**

- Display these words/phrases/clauses and ask pupils to invent silly sentences (or more than one sentence if necessary) using them, e.g. *The reason our cat is fat is that she eats one buffalo a day; When I hear Kylie Minogue, my hair turns purple.*

- Use the examples to discuss how the constructions work, appropriate punctuation, and any other issues, e.g. the accepted standard form is *the reason...*, not *the reason **why**...*

- Collect the best silly sentences and ask pupils to illustrate them to make into wall posters.

- Display the posters with the causal words and punctuation highlighted. Encourage pupils to use these constructions as models in explanatory writing.

Year 5 explanation writing

NLS text-level references

T2 reading: 15, investigate explanatory texts, especially impersonal style and sequential, causal, logical connectives

T2 writing: 22, plan, compose, edit and refine short explanatory texts, using reading as a source, focusing on clarity, conciseness and impersonal style.

NLS sentence-level links

T2: differences between spoken and written language; constructing sentences in different ways.

NLS word-level links

T2: search for, define, and spell technical words in other subjects.

Content and organisation

- Discuss how audience and purpose affect the layout, presentation, structure and organisation of explanation texts, as covered in Year 4.
- Choose a process familiar to pupils from another curricular area and, with the class, compile a flowchart/diagram to illustrate it. Discuss how the organisational features mentioned above might be used in writing up the explanation.

Language features

- Revision of key features: use the example text on page 49 to revise language features covered in Year 4 – generalised language (present tense, third person); sequential links; causal connectives and constructions; technical vocabulary.
- Spoken and written language; impersonal style: cover the text and ask pupils to explain particular parts of it in their own words. (If possible tape-record these to hear again.) Contrast spoken and written versions, and discuss why they differ.
  - Spoken language takes place in a shared context, often interactive, where the speaker can use gesture, intonation and references to pictures, etc. to convey meaning; written explanations require conciseness, clarity and organisation (often into complex sentences).
  - Spoken language is personal and therefore informal; written explanations must be more authoritative and therefore impersonal (e.g. passive voice).

Clear, concise, and informative

- Ask pupils in groups to collect at least six reasonably familiar technical terms from geography, history, science, maths, PE, music.

- Pairs of pupils should then take a word each, and provide both a glossary definition and a sentence which uses the word in context.

- Try a quiz, group against group, in which pupils read out their definitions and sentences, but with the word bleeped out, for others to guess.

- While using the example text to investigate the language of explanation texts (see above), focus on technical terminology and the ways the author explains the meaning of technical words used within the text (see 'Technical terminology' on page 51).

- Look for further techniques for ensuring clarity in other examples of explanation text.

- Ask pupils to return to their own definitions and sentences. Can they integrate their definition into their sentence (shortening and simplifying it if necessary)?

Year 6 explanation writing

NLS text-level references

T3 reading: 15, secure understanding of the features of explanatory text; 16, formal, impersonal language; 19, review a range of text types

T3 writing: 20, impersonal writing; 22, select appropriate style and form for purpose and audience.

NLS sentence-level links

T1, T2: active and passive verbs; complex sentences

T2: formal language

T3: revise language conventions and grammatical features of different text types, including explanatory text.

Content and organisation

Continue to revise organisational features (see Years 4 and 5) in shared reading, and check comprehension by converting the text into a flowchart/diagram. Use flowcharts/diagrams of processes from other subject areas to provide content for explanatory writing.

Language features

- Active and passive: demonstrate **orally** how to convert passive sentences (e.g. *These two gases are carried round the body in the blood*) into the active (*The blood carries these two gases round the body*) and vice versa (active: *Veins carry blood to the heart*; passive: *Blood is carried to the heart by veins*). Ask pupils to try the same activity with silly made-up sentences. Discuss how the passive contributes to explanations.
  - It is more impersonal and thus more authoritative.
  - You can avoid reference to the agent of an action (*The plant was watered regularly*), whereas in the active the agent must be stated (*We watered the plant.*)
- Formal language: see pages 38 and 51.

Explanation checklist

Organisation

- Is there a clear title which introduces the process to be explained? ❏
- If appropriate, are there clear sections with subheadings? ❏
- Does the text open with a general statement, introducing the topic? ❏
- Is there a series of logical steps, explaining the process? ❏
- If possible, is this in time order? ❏
- Have you used organisational devices such as bullet points where appropriate? ❏
- Are well-labelled diagrams used where appropriate to make the meaning clear? ❏
- Is the explanation supported by the positioning of paragraph breaks? ❏
- Is there a closing statement, bringing the explanation to a satisfactory conclusion? ❏

Language features

- Is the text consistently in the present tense? ❏
- Is the text impersonal and authoritative – written in the third person, with use of the passive where appropriate? ❏
- Are there time connectives and other devices to show the sequential structure? ❏
- Is technical terminology used clearly and concisely and, where necessary, defined for the audience? ❏
- Are causal connectives and other devices used to show cause and effect? ❏

Unit 5 – Persuasion text

Purpose: to argue the case for a point of view.

Example: an editorial from a spoof newspaper.

Text structure

- opening statement of the case to be argued
- arguments, given in the form of point plus elaboration
- elaboration may be evidence, explanation, examples
- conclusion: reiteration of the case and summary of the points
- skeleton framework – **pronged bullet points**.

Language features

- present tense
- usually generic participants
- logical language constructions and connectives
- persuasive devices, often including emotive and rhetorical language.

Key teaching points

- Persuasion covers a wide range of text types, from a simple (and highly visual) advertisement to a carefully argued letter of complaint. All, however, conform to the **point + elaboration** format. In the advertisement the point is probably made with a visual image or a slogan, and elaboration consists of design, colour, wordplay and so on. In the letter of complaint the elaboration may be:
  - further details or explanation
  - evidence or argument
  - examples.

- When reading persuasion text, pupils should be alerted to the difference between fact and opinion and encouraged to question writers' presentation of 'facts' and use of persuasive devices (see page 59). They should also be aware of fact and opinion in composing their own arguments.

- When writing persuasion text, pupils should consider what they want their readers to do as a result of reading the piece. A clear idea of a projected outcome clarifies planning.

- Older pupils benefit from opportunities to research and argue points about which they do not feel strongly, or with which they actually disagree.

Common forms of persuasion text

- advertisement
- catalogue
- travel brochure
- pamphlet from pressure group
- political manifesto
- newspaper or magazine article
- poster or flier
- book blurb
- letter to the editor or editorial.

Big book examples of persuasion text

Issues in the News Longman Pelican
Have Your Say Heinemann Literacy World Stage 2 NF Big Book B
How to Persuade People Heinemann Literacy World Stage 3 NF Big Book B
Big Issues Heinemann Literacy World Stage 4 NF Big Book B
Extinction is Forever Kingscourt
See also 'Recommended books for teachers' on pages 79–80.

Time to give Mary the chop

Last week it was proved beyond any shadow of doubt that Mary Stuart, the former Queen of Scots, has been plotting yet again against the life of our dear queen, Elizabeth. It is clearly difficult for our beloved monarch to consent to her own cousin's death, but after nineteen years of threat and betrayal, surely the time has come to sign Mary's death warrant.

The foolish Queen of Scots was long ago rejected by her own countrymen. During her brief but turbulent reign, Scotland suffered religious unrest, lack of leadership and eventually a bloody civil war. As a result, the Scottish people took away her crown and threw her into prison. When she escaped and fled to England, all Scotland sighed with relief to be rid of her!

Since then Mary has lived under Queen Elizabeth's generous protection – and at the expense of English taxpayers – in comfortable English country houses. She has given nothing in return. On the contrary, she has taken every possible opportunity to plot against Elizabeth's life! Surely such betrayal cannot be tolerated any longer?

Moreover, as long as Mary lives, there will be plots. This woman has always claimed to be the rightful Queen of England, and she has always had the support of the King of Spain, who knows he can make her his puppet. Could any true Englishman want to exchange our wise, generous Elizabeth for this vain, selfish woman? Could anyone want our free, prosperous country to fall under the control of the power-crazed King of Spain?

It is hard for Elizabeth to sign the document that sends her own flesh and blood to the block. Yet sign it she must – for herself, for justice, and for the future of England.

from *The Tudor Times*, 1587

Audience
Newspaper readers (unknown audience). Only the most basic background knowledge can be assumed.

Purpose
To convince readers that Mary Queen of Scots should be executed. This involves:
- gaining their attention
- gaining their trust
- convincing them of the importance of the argument and the rightness of the cause.

Projected outcome
What do I want my audience to do?
Support this point of view; help convince Queen Elizabeth to sign the death warrant.

Mary is trouble
∗
- thrown out of Scotland
- religious probs, war
- forced to abdicate, imprisoned

She has betrayed us
∗
- given home, paid for
- not paid back
- constantly plotting

If plots succeed Spain takes over
∗
- claims the crown. Supported by Philip II
- would be P's puppet.
- England falls to Spain

Organisation and content

Title: newspaper headline (short, snappy, eye-catching – play on words).

Introduction
Paragraph 1: setting out the **argument** (Mary has betrayed Elizabeth again and must die) and the **problem** (Elizabeth is reluctant to have her executed).

Argument
Paragraph 2: point 1 – Mary has already failed Scotland. **Elaboration** = evidence: problems during her reign; Scots threw her out.

Paragraph 3: point 2 – Mary has betrayed Elizabeth (and the English taxpayers). **Elaboration** = explanation: she's been given a home; in return she has plotted against her benefactors.

Paragraph 4: point 3 – as long as Mary lives there will be plots, and if she succeeds the outcome will be terrible. **Elaboration** = contrast between Elizabeth and Mary as queen.

Conclusion
Final paragraph: Reiteration: summary of problem; simplified summary of the arguments.

Time to give Mary the chop

Last week it was proved beyond any shadow of doubt that Mary Stuart, the former Queen of Scots, has been plotting yet again against the life of our dear queen, Elizabeth. It is clearly difficult for our beloved monarch to consent to her own cousin's death, but after nineteen years of threat and betrayal, surely the time has come to sign Mary's death warrant.

The foolish Queen of Scots was long ago rejected by her own countrymen. During her brief but turbulent reign, Scotland suffered religious unrest, lack of leadership and eventually a bloody civil war. As a result, the Scottish people took away her crown and threw her into prison. When she escaped and fled to England, all Scotland sighed with relief to be rid of her!

Since then Mary has lived under Queen Elizabeth's generous protection – and at the expense of English taxpayers – in comfortable English country houses. She has given nothing in return. On the contrary, she has taken every possible opportunity to plot against Elizabeth's life! Surely such betrayal cannot be tolerated any longer?

Moreover, as long as Mary lives, there will be plots. This woman has always claimed to be the rightful Queen of England, and she has always had the support of the King of Spain, who knows he can make her his puppet. Could any true Englishman want to exchange our wise, generous Elizabeth for this vain, selfish woman? Could anyone want our free, prosperous country to fall under the control of the power-crazed King of Spain?

It is hard for Elizabeth to sign the document that sends her own flesh and blood to the block. Yet sign it she must – for herself, for justice, and for the future of England.

from *The Tudor Times*, 1587

How to teach writing across the curriculum at key stage 2 © Sue Palmer   57

Form and style

- persuasion text – a newspaper editorial
- a reasoned argument containing several points, each backed up by evidence or further argument

- persuasive language and logic
- emotive language, to draw the reader along with the cause.

Language features

General language

- Apart from historical references, written in the **present tense**, because the issue is a current one for the writer.
- A mixture of named people (*Mary, Elizabeth, the King of Spain*) and the generalised participants who are affected by their actions (*her own countrymen, English taxpayers, any true Englishman…*).

The language of argument

The argument consists of an opening premise, then three supporting points (see 'Argument' opposite), held together by logical language.

- Complex sentences using **logical connectives** of the *if…then* type (**after** *nineteen years… the time has come…*; **When** *she escaped…all Scotland must…*).
- **Connectives** between sentences showing logical relationships:
  – *As a result* indicates cause and effect
  – *On the contrary…; Yet….* showing this sentence will state something in opposition to the preceding one.
  – *Moreover* moves us on to a further level of argument, built on what has gone before.
- The use of **hypothesis** (*When she escaped…all Scotland must have sighed; Could any true Englishman want…?*).

Persuasive devices

Persuasive language does not usually rely just on argument to make the case: it uses language to drag the reader along. Often this involves **disguising opinion as fact**.

- The use of value-laden **adjectives** (*dear queen, beloved monarch, foolish Queen, turbulent reign, power-crazed King of Spain*).
- Use of **emotive words**, highly charged with emotional meaning (*threat, betrayal, suffered, puppet*).
- **Exaggerated language** (the case against Mary has not just been proved, but *proved beyond any shadow of doubt*; Mary didn't just *plot* but *has taken every possible opportunity to plot*).
- Use of constructions which **dare you to disagree** (*surely the time has come…*). When the author asks *Could any true Englishman want to exchange…* there is an assumption that anyone who disagrees is not a 'true Englishman'.
- The use of **concession** (*It is clearly difficult for…but…; It is hard for…Yet…*) to counter possible objections.
- **Rhetorical questions** (*Could any…? Could anyone?*).
- **Repetition** for effect (*for herself, for justice, and for the future of England*).

Formal, impersonal language

An editorial requires formal language, suggesting that the arguments have been carefully considered. Formality also helps deflect attention from shaky logic or evidence, and can be used to disguise opinion as fact.

- Written in the **third person**, with no indication of who the author is.
- Occasional use of the **passive voice** (e.g. *it was proved; such betrayal cannot be tolerated*) which is formal and impersonal.
- Use of **formal vocabulary** (e.g. *monarch, Moreover*).

Year 4 persuasion writing

NLS text-level references

T3 reading: 16–18, read, compare, evaluate
arguments; investigate organisation,
language (style and vocabulary); 19,
evaluate adverts

T3 writing: 21–3 plan and present a point of
view, (letter, report, or script), using
writing frame; 25, design an advert
(poster, radio jingle).

NLS sentence-level links

T3: use of connectives to structure argument.

Content and organisation

- Read examples of persuasive writing (see those
listed on page 56) and use the 'pronged-bullet'
skeleton to reduce them to note form: write the
points on the left of the bullet and any
elaboration on the right (see illustration on
page 58).
- Choose a controversial issue with which pupils
are familiar and establish a point of view. Ask
them to list points on a pronged-bullet skeleton.
As you compile them, draw attention to the
various types of elaboration – explanation,
evidence, examples.

Language features

- Style and vocabulary: study examples of
persuasive writing (e.g. page 57) and help
children identify elements of persuasive style,
such as:
  - value-laden and emotive language, chosen to
influence the reader
  - exaggeration and repetition used for effect
  - formal vocabulary and constructions, used to
give an air of authority.
- Use of connectives to structure an argument:
collect examples from reading, e.g. *if...then...;
on the other hand; furthermore; moreover;
therefore; finally*. In shared writing, compose a
persuasive letter from a fictional character (e.g.
Cinderella writing to her sisters to say why she
should go to the ball; the Sheriff of Nottingham
writing to Robin Hood to evict him from the
forest), using as many of the connectives as
possible and demonstrating other aspects of
persuasive style, as above.
- Turn the finished product into a writing frame,
by deleting everything but the connective
devices. Ask pupils, in pairs, to use this to write
the response (e.g. from the sisters or Robin).

No one forgets a good teacher!

Look at a selection of advertisements, from the past (see page 63) and present. Help pupils analyse
these on a pronged-bullet skeleton, for example:

Look at this ad!   ✳ ——

Want this product!   ✳ ——   elaboration here is often in terms of of visual
image, colour, logo, lettering language play
like alliteration, all of which can appeal to
the audience's vanity, conscience, or sense
of humour

✳ —

Buy it!

Discuss the many ways advertisers manipulate their audience. Ask children in pairs to use the skeleton to
plan their own advertising campaign (e.g. for a school event or an imaginary product) – consisting of a
poster and a radio advertisement with a jingle.

Year 5 persuasion writing

NLS text-level references

T3 reading: 12–14 read, evaluate 'letters to the editor', newspaper comment, ads, fliers for layout, language, clarity, informative content (fact/opinion); 15, collect and investigate persuasive devices

T3 writing: 17, write group letters for real purposes; 18, write commentary (e.g. editorial) on an issue; 19, construct and present an argument to the class, and evaluate.

NLS sentence-level links

T3: writing for different purposes and audiences.

Content and organisation

- Read a collection of 'letters to the editor' on current local and national issues. Revise the use of the pronged-bullet skeleton to make notes on the main points in these letters, and how each point is elaborated. Evaluate how well the writers have made their points and backed them up. Make a skeleton plan for a letter to the editor on an issue of interest to the pupils.
- Read our persuasion example (see page 57) and plan a similar editorial on a controversial issue in any historical period with which the pupils are familiar. Make a skeleton plan which can be used later as the basis of writing.

Language features

- Persuasive devices. Study the use of persuasive devices in our example, and list the devices, with short extracts to illustrate them. Ask pupils to use the constructions to compose single sentences of their own, related to a frivolous topic, e.g.

our dear queen... beloved monarch → *our beloved Scotch terrier...much-loved pet*

has taken every possible opportunity to plot → *has taken every possible opportunity to let us know that he is bored. Surely the time has come to take him for a walk... Could any true animal-lover deny him an outing? Could anyone keep this dog penned up for a moment longer...?*

Presenting persuasion

- Organise a balloon debate. Each pupil chooses a character, alive or dead, whose case he or she would like to argue. Pupils research their characters, and make skeleton notes (minimum of three points, each with elaboration) on why their lives should be spared.
- Pupils should then write a speech, using a range of persuasive devices (as above), pleading their character's case.
- In groups of three, and in the role of their character, pupils enter the balloon. While flying high above the earth, the balloon's hot-air system fails, and two people must be sacrificed so that one can be saved.
- Each character gives a speech arguing his or her claim to live. (Most pupils will speak better if they work from their skeleton notes. The experience of writing the speech should improve use of language, especially if they stay in role.)
- On the basis of the speech, the rest of the class each write down the name of one person who must be sacrificed (secret ballot to avoid embarrassment). The survivor's name is then announced.
- If it goes well, you can have play-offs between the various survivors.

Year 6 persuasion writing

NLS text-level references

T2 reading: recognise how effective arguments are constructed, including pre-empting and answering potential objections

T3 writing: construct effective arguments.

NLS sentence-level links

T2: conventions of formal language; use of conditionals.

Content and organisation

- Read a range of persuasion texts (see those listed on page 56) and identify the arguments for and against particular positions. Help pupils make skeleton notes of these arguments on a for-and-against grid. Note only the main points, not the elaboration.
- Discuss a controversial issue, e.g. hunting, homework, the three- or four-term school year. Create a grid skeleton for points on either side.
- Ask pupils to choose one side or the other, and turn it into a skeleton for a piece of persuasive writing – i.e. add elaboration to each point (including, where relevant, pre-empting or answering potential objections).

Language features

- See Year 6 discussion writing (page 68). Pupils should then use their persuasion skeletons as the basis for a piece of discussion writing.

Persuasive writing checklist

Organisation

- Does the introductory paragraph contain a clear statement of the case to be argued? ❑
- Does it also contain any background information required by the reader to understand the issue? ❑
- Is each argument clearly stated, preferably with a paragraph to itself? ❑
- Is each argument backed up by any information necessary for the reader to understand? ❑
- Is each argument supported by some form of evidence or examples? ❑
- Does the piece end with a restatement of the case and a summary of the main points? ❑

Language features

- Is the text consistently in the present tense (apart from historical references)? ❑
- Does it contain logical language constructions and connectives? ❑
- Does it contain an appropriate range of persuasive devices to affect the reader, such as:
    - powerful adjectives and other emotive words ❑
    - constructions such as *Surely…; It is clear that…; Everyone knows that…* ❑
    - the use of questions to make a point ❑
    - repetition for effect. ❑
- Does the text take opportunities, where appropriate, to answer any likely arguments on the opposite side? ❑

Advertisements

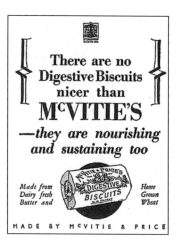

There are no
Digestive Biscuits
nicer than
McVITIE'S
—they are nourishing
and sustaining too

Made from
Dairy fresh
Butter and

Home
Grown
Wheat

MADE BY McVITIE & PRICE

Milko!

CREAMY
MILK
Chocolate

RICH
Chocolate
CREAM

Milko! There's nothing
like a penguin. Covered
with the creamiest milk
chocolate you ever tasted.
Only 3½d for the biggest
milk chocolate treat there
is. Look for the bright red,
green or blue foil wrappers
when you're shopping.
Have a penguin to-day.

chocolate
Penguin

CRUNCHY
chocolate
biscuit

from Macdonalds of Glasgow
who bake the best biscuits

OVALTINE
*The World's Best
Nightcap*

A CUP of 'Ovaltine' at bedtime helps to relax
nervous tensions and promote the conditions favourable to natural, refreshing sleep.
Made from Nature's best foods, its valuable
nutritive properties, including additional vita-
mins, assist in providing the nourishment to
restore the tired body and rebuild strength
and vitality.

For these reasons delicious 'Ovaltine' has long
been the regular bedtime beverage in countless
homes throughout the world. There is nothing
like it.

*No other beverage
can give you better sleep*

1/6, 2/6 and 4/6 per tin

P.909A

FRY'S MILK CHOCOLATE

DESPERATION. PACIFICATION. EXPECTATION. ACCLAMATION. REALIZATION.
"IT'S FRY'S"

J.S. FRY & SONS Lᵗᴰ BRISTOL & LONDON.

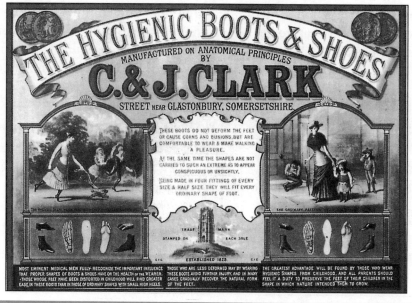

THE HYGIENIC BOOTS & SHOES
MANUFACTURED ON ANATOMICAL PRINCIPLES
BY
C.& J. CLARK
STREET NEAR GLASTONBURY, SOMERSETSHIRE.

THESE BOOTS DO NOT DEFORM THE FEET
OR CAUSE CORNS AND BUNIONS, BUT ARE
COMFORTABLE TO WEAR & MAKE WALKING
A PLEASURE.

AT THE SAME TIME THE SHAPES ARE NOT
CARRIED TO SUCH AN EXTREME AS TO APPEAR
CONSPICUOUS OR UNSIGHTLY.

BEING MADE IN FOUR FITTINGS OF EVERY
SIZE & HALF SIZE THEY WILL FIT EVERY
ORDINARY SHAPE OF FOOT.

TRADE MARK
STAMPED ON EACH SOLE

ESTABLISHED 1825.

MOST EMINENT MEDICAL MEN FULLY RECOGNIZE THE IMPORTANT INFLUENCE
THAT PROPER SHAPES OF BOOTS & SHOES HAVE ON THE HEALTH OF THE WEARER.
THOSE WHOSE FEET HAVE BEEN DISTORTED IN CHILDHOOD WILL FIND GREATER
EASE IN THESE BOOTS THAN IN THOSE OF ORDINARY SHAPES WITH SMALL HIGH HEELS.

THOSE WHO ARE LESS DEFORMED MAY BY WEARING
THESE BOOTS AVOID FURTHER INJURY, AND IN MANY
CASES GRADUALLY RECOVER THE NATURAL FORM
OF THE FEET.

THE GREATEST ADVANTAGE WILL BE FOUND BY THOSE WHO WEAR
HYGIENIC SHAPES FROM CHILDHOOD, AND ALL PARENTS SHOULD
FEEL IT A DUTY TO PRESERVE THE FEET OF THEIR CHILDREN IN THE
SHAPE IN WHICH NATURE INTENDED THEM TO GROW.

Unit 6 – Discussion text

Purpose: to present arguments and information from different viewpoints.

Example: an answer to an essay question.

Text structure

- opens with clear statement of the issue under discussion
- one of two types of organisation:
  - arguments for + supporting evidence
    arguments against + supporting evidence
  - argument/counter-argument, presented one point at a time
- arguments supported by evidence and/or examples
- reader must be clear which side argues which point
- skeleton framework – a for-and-against grid.

Language features

- generally present tense, third person
- formal, impersonal style
- logical language constuctions and connectives
- connectives/language constructions to show shifts from one point of view to the other.

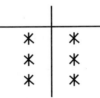

Key teaching points

- The ability to write discussion text builds on children's persuasive writing. When they can argue one side of a case, they are ready to put both. Discussion, however, uses less subjective, value-laden and emotive language than persuasion.

- In everyday life, writers are more often concerned to convey their own point of view than to give a balanced appraisal. Some apparent discussion texts often turn out to be persuasion in disguise (as, possibly, in our example opposite).

- The most likely place to meet discussion is in exams, assessing pupils' ability to produce reasoned argument. Much discussion, therefore, is in the shape of formal essays (see notes on page 69).

- In a short discussion text, like our example, it is best to make all the points for one side then all the points for the other. In a longer discussion, argument and counter-argument may be interwoven, but paragraphing and connectives like *On the other hand...* must ensure the two viewpoints are clearly delineated.

Common forms of persuasion text

- newspaper editorial
- non-fiction book on an 'issue'
- exam answer in secondary or tertiary education
- write-up of a debate
- formal essay
- leaflet or article giving balanced account of an issue.

Big book examples of persuasion text

Issues in the News Longman Pelican

Big Issues Heinemann Literacy World Stage 4 NF Big Book B

Viewpoints on Waste Rigby Magic Bean

See also 'Recommended books for teachers' on pages 79–80.

Do we still need zoos?

Zoos were originally set up so that people could see and learn about wild animals from distant lands. As more people became city-dwellers, never seeing animals in the wild, zoos began to house local creatures too. However, in today's world, are zoos really necessary?

Since people can now see any sort of wild animal in its natural habitat, simply by tuning in to a TV programme or buying a video, some animal rights activists claim that zoos are out of date. They argue that it is cruel to capture animals, transport them long distances, and then keep them caged up, simply for the entertainment of human beings. Captive animals often develop 'zoochosis' – abnormal behaviour like rocking or swaying – which indicates that they are bored and unhappy in their prison-like conditions.

On the other hand, there is a huge difference between watching an animal on screen and seeing it in real life. It could be argued that visiting a zoo is educational, often increasing people's concern for wildlife and conservation, which is of great importance in today's developing – and often overdeveloped – world. Indeed, sometimes the only way to save an endangered species may be to arrange for it to breed in captivity. Behind the scenes, zoos also provide scientists with opportunities to research into animal behaviour: modern zoos can therefore be much better planned than old-fashioned ones, providing animals with carefully designed enclosures appropriate to their needs.

It seems, then, that there are still arguments for retaining zoos. These should, however, be carefully planned with the animals' welfare in mind: in the modern world, there is no excuse for keeping animals in cramped or cruel conditions.

Audience

Readers who are interested in the topic and want to know the facts on either side. (Or, possibly, a teacher or examiner who wants to know how well the writer understands the issue.)

Purpose

1. to set out the main arguments on both sides of the case

2. to come to a reasoned conclusion, based on the facts.

Against zoos		For zoos	
Don't need any more ✳	original for people to see animals / now have TV, video	TV not as good as real life ✳	zoos educational / increase people's interest in animals
Cruel ✳	catch, transport, cage / zoochosis / just for entertainment	Conservation ✳	endangered species breed in zoos
		Not cruel ✳	scientists can research in zoos / well-planned enclosures

Organisation and content

Title: a question summing up the issue under debate. Terms of discussion defined: three key words – *still, need* and *zoos* – suggest that zoos were once necessary, but things may have changed.

Introduction

Paragraph 1: draws attention to key words, clarifying the reason zoos were set up, and reiterating the question.

Argument

Paragraph 2: the argument against zoos
1. first sentence states why zoos are no longer needed to perform the function defined in the introduction (argument 1)
2. second sentence gives a reason for disbanding them (argument 2)
3. third sentence elaborates this point (scientific evidence).

Paragraph 3: the argument in favour of zoos
1. first sentence contests argument 1
2. second sentence elaborates, converting the argument into an up-to-date reason for maintaining zoos
3. third sentence elaborates this new argument (further detail)
4. fourth and fifth sentences contest argument 2 (point plus elaboration).

Conclusion

Final paragraph: concluding statement
1. first sentence provides an answer to the question posed in the title, based on argument 1
2. second sentence sums up the implications of argument 2.

Do we still need zoos?

Zoos were originally set up so that people could see and learn about wild animals from distant lands. As more people became city-dwellers, never seeing animals in the wild, zoos began to house local creatures too. However, in today's world, are zoos really necessary?

Since people can now see any sort of wild animal in its natural habitat, simply by tuning in to a TV programme or buying a video, some animal rights activists claim that zoos are out of date. They argue that it is cruel to capture animals, transport them long distances, and then keep them caged up, simply for the entertainment of human beings. Captive animals often develop 'zoochosis' – abnormal behaviour like rocking or swaying – which indicates that they are bored and unhappy in their prison-like conditions.

On the other hand, there is a huge difference between watching an animal on screen and seeing it in real life. It could be argued that visiting a zoo is educational, often increasing people's concern for wildlife and conservation, which is of great importance in today's developing – and often overdeveloped – world. Indeed, sometimes the only way to save an endangered species may be to arrange for it to breed in captivity. Behind the scenes, zoos also provide scientists with opportunities to research into animal behaviour: modern zoos can therefore be much better planned than old-fashioned ones, providing animals with carefully designed enclosures appropriate to their needs.

It seems, then, that there are still arguments for retaining zoos. These should, however, be carefully planned with the animals' welfare in mind: in the modern world, there is no excuse for keeping animals in cramped or cruel conditions.

65

Form and style

- discussion text – general, impersonal, formal essay
- terms of discussion must be clearly defined
- two sides of an argument clearly set out
- layout must reflect the argument – paragraphs.

Language features

General language

- Apart from historical references, written in the **present tense**, because the issue is a current one.
- References to *people, activists, scientists, animals, wildlife*, etc. (generalised participants), because this is a general argument, not just about one particular zoo.

Formal, impersonal language

Dicussions call for formal written language patterns, indicating that the arguments have been carefully considered and composed. They also require an impersonal stance: the personal opinions of the the writer are unimportant.

- Written in the **third person** using generalised 'voices' for the two sides of the debate (e.g. *activists – they*).
- Occasional use of the **passive voice** (e.g. *It could be argued*) which is formal and impersonal, and avoids the question of who exactly is arguing the point.
- Frequent use of **formal vocabulary** (e.g. *originally* rather than *first*; *habitat* rather than *home*; *indicates* rather than *shows*). On the whole, formal vocabulary has its roots in the classical languages and is associated with written language and formal situations. The simpler words we associate with speech and directness tend to have Old English origins.
- Frequent use of **complex sentences** (see 'The language of ideas' opposite) which are a feature of formal written language.

The language of ideas

- Discussions are often about abstract ideas, so many of the terms used are **abstract nouns** (things you can neither see or touch), e.g.

entertainment, zoochosis, difference, concern, conservation, importance, captivity, welfare.

- **Complex sentences** often show the logical relationships between the ideas expressed in clauses, e.g. in the first two paragraphs the **conjunctions** *so that..., As...,* and *Since...* all show cause and effect.
- **Connectives** between sentences also show logical relationships:
  – *However...* and *On the other hand...* both indicate that an alternative viewpoint is about to be expressed
  – *Indeed...* suggests an accumulation of facts
  – *Therefore...* indicates cause and effect
  – *Then...* near the beginning of the final paragraph suggests that we have arrived at a logical conclusion.
- **Punctuation** can also be used to indicate links between ideas: the **semicolon** in the final sentence of paragraph 3 and the **colon** in the last sentence of the final paragraph both suggest causal links.
- The use of the **conditional form** of the verb (*It could be argued..., may be to...*) indicates that the writer is dealing in hypothesis. It also distances the author from the argument.

Expressing both sides of the debate

- **Paragraph breaks** are used to help show the division between the two points of view.
- Generalised terms are used to indicate **general participants** on one side of the debate, e.g. *some animal rights activists claim...*
- The **passive voice** (*It could be argued...*) is used in the same way to indicate the opposing view.
- Connectives like *However...* and *On the other hand...* show that an opposing view is about to be voiced.

Year 6 discussion writing

NLS text-level references

T2 reading: 15, 16, construction of effective arguments, features of balanced arguments

T2 writing: 18, 19, construct effective arguments, write balanced report of controversial issue

T3 reading: 16, impersonal formal language; 19, review a range of text types

T3 writing: 22, select appropriate style and form for purpose and audience.

NLS sentence-level links

T2:   formal language; conditional verb forms

T3:   formal, impersonal writing; complex sentences; language conventions of discursive texts.

Content and organisation

- Read examples of discussion text (see sample text on page 65 and those listed on page 64) and help pupils convert them into skeleton notes, i.e. a for-and-against grid, with pronged bullets (point plus elaboration) on each side.
- Investigate the organisation of the text (see page 66) and in each case establish which type of construction the author has chosen:
  - arguments for + supporting evidence/ arguments against + supporting evidence
  - argument/counter-argument presented one point at a time.
- Create skeleton notes for a discussion piece on a topic familiar to pupils.

Conditional language

*If all the world **were** paper, and all the sea*
*   **were** ink,*
And all the trees were bread and cheese,
*   what **would** we have to drink?*

Make a collection of conditional constructions used in discussion texts, e.g. *It **could** be claimed that... This **might** mean that... It is **possible** that... This would **perhaps** result in...*

Establish that much argument is hypothetical; authors should use conditional constructions when making statements for which they have no evidence. Conditional language involves some changes to the verb form (notably *will → would*, but also, if you're being pernickety, *was → were*, as in the traditional rhyme above).

Ask pupils to use sentence starts like the ones above to create sentences about familiar subjects. Do this orally first until they are familiar with the conditional constructions and verb forms. Then integrate it into shared and supported writing activities.

Language features

- Language conventions of discursive texts; formal, impersonal language. Use the example texts to discuss general features of discussion language (see page 67 and checklist). If necessary, create a writing frame (see the example on page 72).
- Complex sentences; formal, impersonal language.
  - Take some complex sentences from an example text, e.g. *Since people can now see any sort of wild animal in its natural habitat... some animal rights activists claim that zoos are out of date.*
  - Then turn them into a mini-writing frame: *Since... some ... activists claim that...*
  - Demonstrate, then ask children in pairs to make up sentences on other topics that fit into the frame, e.g. ***Since** aeroplanes cause much more damage to the ozone layer than cars, **some** environmental **activists claim** that there should be much higher taxation on air travel.*
  - These sentences should be rehearsed orally, so that pupils become used to articulating complex sentence constructions and the language of argument.

Discussion checklist

Organisation

- Does the introductory paragraph clearly state the issue under discussion, picking up any key words from the title? ❏
- Are the arguments on each side of the debate clearly stated? ❏
- Is each argument supported by evidence, explanation, or examples? ❏
- Do the paragraph breaks help the reader clearly see both sides of the argument? ❏
- Is there a final paragraph in which a conclusion is reached, based on the arguments? ❏

Language features

- Is the text consistently in the present tense (apart from historical references)? ❏
- Are the arguments presented in the third person, using:
  - generalised voices (e.g. *Some people claim…*)? ❏
  - the passive voice (e.g. *It is argued that…*)? ❏
- Does the text use formal, impersonal language and vocabulary? ❏
- Are links made clear by the use of logical connectives (e.g. *Therefore, Consequently*) and connectives showing the onset of an alternative viewpoint (e.g. *On the other hand…* or *However…*)? ❏
- Is there use of conditional language (*It may be…* or *It could be…*) to suggest possibility or hypothesis? ❏

Formal essays

The most common form of discussion writing is the formal essay, and this doesn't crop up very often in everyday life – it tends to be something you do as part of school work or examinations. The **audience** for formal essays, therefore, is usually a teacher or an exam marker, and the **purpose** is to impress them that you know:

- all the facts about the subject
- how to structure a formal essay.

This is not a very natural writing situation! The checklist below will help you make a good job of it.

When writing a formal essay or exam question

- Carefully state the issue under discussion, attending to the terms of reference (i.e. what are the key words in the title?).

- Make points clearly and provide plenty of elaboration (explanatory detail, supporting evidence, examples) – do not wander off the point.

- Keep **for** and **against** arguments clearly separated (see next bullet point).

- Return to the issue at the end, summarising the main points and, if required, offering an answer to the question, based on the arguments.

- Remember that the person marking the essay is not interested in your opinion, but in how well you know the facts and are able to argue the case.

Teaching non-fiction writing

Audience + Purpose → Form and style

The 'equation' above sums up the process of planning a piece of writing. The experienced writer assesses each element almost instantaneously, but children need time to think and consider, so that the process will become similarly automatic for them.

Always take time to discuss the four key questions:

1. **Audience** – for whom is it intended (and what do we know about them)?
2. **Purpose** – what is the purpose of this particular piece of writing?
3. **Form** – how will these two facts affect the form of the writing?
4. **Style** – how will they affect the style?

Audience

The form and style of a piece of writing vary considerably depending on the audience, e.g. is the audience

- yourself? → you know exactly how much detail is required, and can dispense with formalities
- a personal friend or friends? → you have a good idea how much background detail is necessary, and can write informally
- a person or people you don't know personally, but whom you know something about (e.g. age, interests, the level of background knowledge they are likely to have)? → you can probably

gauge how much background information is necessary, and how explicit you have to be but your style will be reasonably formal
- a remote and unknown audience? → writing must be explicit and probably formal.

Encourage pupils always to consider the exact audience for whom they are about to write and to think how it will affect their approach and style.

Purpose

The general purpose will determine the text type and structure, depending on whether you want to:

- retell events → **recount**
- decribe the characteristics of something → **report**
- tell someone how to do or make something → **instruction**
- explain how or why something happens → **explanation**
- persuade someone to agree with your point of view → **persuasion**
- present a balanced argument → **discussion**.

But each individual piece of writing will also have a more specific purpose. The purpose of each of our example texts is given on the analysis page. Encourage children to think clearly about the specific purpose of any writing they are intending, and to consider how it will affect the form.

Form

There are a number of obvious forms writing can take depending upon purpose. As part of their writing across the curriculum, you will probably want pupils to produce books (or sections of books), booklets, essays and various other kinds of written accounts. On the first page of each text unit, we list a selection of forms of writing which are typical of the text type.

The National Literacy Strategy requires children to tackle a number of forms during Key Stage 2, each of which has associated conventions, both organisational and linguistic:

- personal communication – letters, notes, messages, telegrams
- journalistic writing – newspaper reports, editorials, obituaries
- note-taking and making – lists, notes, charts and other formats
- publicity material – posters, jingles, leaflets, pamphlets
- formal documents – CVs, police reports, school reports.

There is guidance on major conventions on pages 72–3, but since conventions are best established by discussion of a variety of example texts, it is helpful to build up your own portfolio. The anthologised materials listed on page 80 include many examples.

Another aspect of form is **presentation**. Children need to consider layout and organisation of material on the page, and to select appropriately from the wide range of presentational devices available to them, including:

- headings and subheadings
- bullet points
- numbering
- use of diagrams and other graphic organisers
- boxes and various attention-grabbing devices.

All of these are covered within the text-unit teaching pages.

Style

To some extent, style must be a personal thing – even in non-fiction writing, we wish to encourage pupils to find their own 'voice' and to make decisions about approach and tone. But many elements of style are determined by audience, purpose and form. For instance, every piece of writing must find a place somewhere along the following continua:

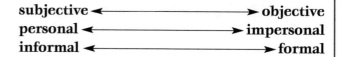

The position on each continuum has an effect on vocabulary, sentence construction and other grammatical elements, as illustrated in the analysis of language features in each text unit. Children must be aware of the significance of these factors and able to adjust their own use of language as appropriate.

Conventions of form and style

Personal communication – letters

When children are producing a hand-written letter, it is best to stick to tried-and-tested conventions.

The format below is typical of a business letter produced on a word processor. The general convention is to align everything, apart from the writer's contact details, on the left and to use minimal punctuation.

The Castle,
Cloud Lane,
Once upon a time
15th April, 1002

Dear Jack,
    Any chance of getting my hen back? I miss her.
    Hope you and your mother are well.

        Best wishes,
        Ernie Ogre.

Beanstalk Enterprises Ltd
21–35 Cottage Row
Once-Upon-A-Time
Tel: 04463 929292 Fax: 04463 929286

Mr E. Ogre
The Castle
Once-Upon-A-Time

17 April 1002

Dear Mr Ogre,

Thank you for your letter of 3 April…

able to come to some satisfactory arrangement.

Yours sincerely,

Jack Twankey

Jack Twankey
Managing Director

Writing frames

Writing frames are an extremely useful way of familiarising pupils with aspects of form and style. Lewis and Wray's book of sample frames (see page 79), from which this illustration is taken, is an invaluable teaching aid. However, the best writing frames are those which you create yourself to fit a particular piece of writing, in a particular form, perhaps focusing on a particular aspect of style.

Once you are familiar with writing frames, you can easily produce your own, based on the model texts you investigate with children.

Some people think that

because

They argue that

Another group that agrees with this point of view is

They say that

On the other hand .... disagree with the idea that

They claim that

They also say

My opinion is

because

Journalistic writing – newspaper reports, editorials, obituaries

Collect examples of a variety of papers, national and local, including broadsheets, tabloids and redtops. The best model for most children's journalistic writing is probably an upmarket tabloid but only broadsheets publish conventional obituaries.

Note-taking and making

This book does not deal specifically with the teaching of note-taking but the making of skeleton notes is an essential component of the teaching sequence suggested.

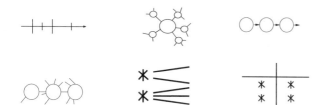

Publicity material – advertisements, posters, jingles, leaflets

Advertising material varies considerably depending upon content, so you need a wide variety of examples. Fortunately, collecting them makes a very good homework exercise. For example

> Find and bring to school:
> - an advertisement from a newspaper or magazine
> - a copy of a poster advertisement you find effective
> - a radio jingle
> - an advertising leaflet.

Formal documents – CVs, police reports, school reports

Most teachers should be able to find samples of CVs and school reports. The police report form below is based on a genuine document (this would be A4 size).

ROSSETDALE CONSTABULARY
WITNESS STATEMENT FORM
(J Act 1967 S.9 MC Act 1980, S 102 MC Rules)

Form MG11

Statement of ....

Age if under 21............ (If over 21, insert 'over 21')

Occupation ....

This statement (consisting of........pages, each signed by me) is true to the best of my knowledge and belief and I make it knowing that, if it is tendered in evidence, I shall be liable to prosecution if I have wilfully stated in it anything which I know to be false or do not believe to be true.

Dated the ....day of ....20..........

Signature ....

Signature... Signature witnessed by ....

Shared, guided and independent writing

Most children do not learn to write naturally. As this book has demonstrated, there is a great deal involved in producing an effective piece of writing. A few lucky children – fluent readers with excellent memory skills – are able to internalise the appropriate patterns of written language naturally. In the past, however, the majority of children failed to acquire the necessary technical knowledge and gave up the ghost, or resorted to simply copying out information from books.

The text units in this book summarise what children need to know in order to produce writing for a variety of audiences and purposes. The knowledge and skills (along with other general word and sentence level skills) must be taught gradually, and regularly revisited throughout the primary years. However, knowledge and skills are no use unless they are exercised in context. When children have learned something new about how to write, they need immediate opportunities:

- to see how that new learning can be integrated within the act of writing, preferably for a real purpose
- to try it out for themselves, again within a meaningful context.

Teaching about writing should always lead immediately into shared, guided and independent writing activities.

Shared writing

Demonstration	Scribing	Supported writing
Model the process of writing for the children. Write a section of text on the board or flipchart, and keep up a constant commentary* on what you are doing and why. Demonstrate exactly how the ideas get out of your head and on to the page. It is almost impossible to compose and commentate at the same time. You need a script – work it out beforehand.	Use scribing to pull the class in, especially if they're beginning to shuffle, or if there's an opportunity to follow up the day's objectives. Invite the class to contribute ideas, forms of words, alternative constructions, etc. Choose the most successful and integrate them into the demonstration, still keeping up the commentary.	Every so often, ask pairs of pupils to work on a section of text together. Ensure they understand the content and the language features concerned. The best supported writing tasks involve putting one or more of the day's learning objectives into immediate practice. Give a time limit, then ask for feedback – and proceed as for scribing.

* Use our text analysis pages to plan your commentary. Select grammatical concepts appropriate to the age group.

How do I integrate shared writing lessons with cross-curricular writing?

If it's something specific, such as how to write an introductory paragraph, demonstrate it on an appropriate piece of cross-curricular writing (e.g. 'The Battle of Salamis'), leaving pupils to finish the write-up in independent writing.

You can use the skeleton here to save time. Divide up the paragraphs/sections between pairs/groups of pupils, and ask them to write their own paragraph in independent writing. Make a composite piece from the best submissions. In a subsequent lesson, discuss and edit to improve content and coherence.

At a later date, give pupils the chance to try out what they've learned from your demonstration on another similar piece of writing (e.g. 'The Battle of Marathon'): this time they could complete the whole piece.

If it's a more general objective, such as the use of organisational devices, choose one section for shared writing (make sure it's not always the opening paragraph) and ask pupils to write the rest.

The decision on whether to divide this up between groups or let all pupils complete the whole piece depends on whether there is another complete piece of this type that you want them to write in the future.

Successful supported writing

- Don't leave children to choose their own partners: many mess about if they are working with a chum. Allocate 'writing partners' (and constantly revise them if they don't work), based on pupils who have something to offer each other (e.g. a bright dyslexic and a competent plodder).

- Spend time training pupils into this routine:

  Rehearse   Work out what you're going to write orally first. Listen to how it sounds, and improve it if you can.

  Write   Either one writes while the other helps, or both write their own version (the latter can save squabbles). This is another opportunity to edit as you go.

  Read   Read it through and see how it sounds. Read the whole of the shared piece, with your bit on the end, and see how it sounds. Again, edit if necessary.

- Give a short time limit and emphasise the urgency of the task. You can adjust the time limit if necessary, but you don't want pupils thinking there's time to waste.

Independent writing

Two types of teaching objective may be met during independent writing.

- Specific **literacy objectives**, of the type described in the teaching units. Once children have watched you put a new skill into practice in shared writing, they need an opportunity to try it out themselves. Depending on the objective and the writing task, you may use one or both of the following:
  – a supervised supported writing task (see pages 74–5)
  – a highly focused independent writing task (approximately 20–30 mins) immediately after the shared lesson.
- **Cross-curricular objectives** – recording knowledge acquired in another curriculum area. This is likely to be more time-consuming than a specific literacy objective. Pupils could begin their own writing as part of your literacy work (i.e. following up your shared writing session) and continue during History/ Geography/whatever.

Sometimes, it's possible to achieve both at one fell swoop. If not, decide which is more important, and plan appropriately.

Independent writing is a whole-class activity, so there should not be a 'carousel' of different activities to follow up the shared teaching. If you've just spent quarter of an hour demonstrating how to do something, you don't want some children to go off doing something else. Some pupils, however, require more support than others, and writing tasks must be scaffolded appropriately, e.g. using writing frames, sentence starts, lists of suitable words, etc. Or you may simply ask a less able group to try for themselves the piece of writing you have just demonstrated.

Guided writing

While the whole class is engaged in independent writing, the teacher is free to home in on the specific needs of a group of children. This is an opportunity to provide focused help with those areas of word, sentence, or text level work of particular significance. You may choose to work with a particular ability group (i.e. a reading group), or you may create an *ad hoc* group of children needing help on one aspect of writing. In either case the overall writing task provides a context for focused teaching.

Levels of teaching support

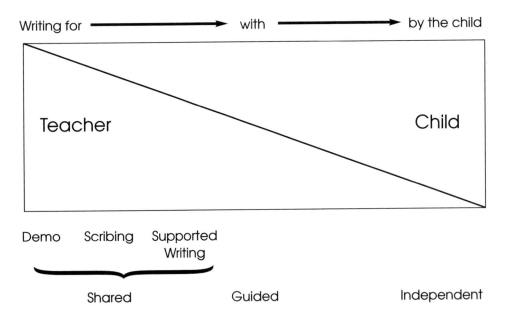

Planning and plenary

The words planning and plenary are linked by more than alliteration. The 'plenary session' at the end of a lesson is the chance to revise its main points which, of course, means returning to your initial teaching objectives.

This book is intended to serve as an overall planning device:

- Use the teaching plan on pages 14–15 to link writing to work across the curriculum. Possible links are suggested on pages 12–13.
- Select specific literacy teaching objectives from the year-by-year teaching pages of the text units.
- Display your main objective(s) for each lesson so pupils are aware of the point of the lesson.

Don't let the plenary drop off the end!

Teaching is a messy business, and no one can ever plan the exact course of a lesson. It's not surprising, therefore, that many teachers have found it difficult to integrate the plenary session into their daily practice. However, research shows very clearly that the chance to **review the main points** is an enormous aid to children's learning. This review is likely to be even more useful if the children are directly involved, and given the chance to **articulate what they have learned**. It's worth making the effort.

- At the very least, take a few minutes to remind pupils of the main points you have covered. Make this review as interactive as possible, for example:

  - go through the displayed objectives and ask pupils whether you can tick each one off
  - ask pupils to suggest what are today's 'key words', and list the best answers on the board (plus any important ones they miss)
  - use an aide-memoire, such as a page from the appropriate *Skeleton Poster Book* (see page 79) that sums up organisational or language features.
  - use the text you have produced during shared writing to remind pupils of the key points by highlighting/annotating.

  This sort of plenary is appropriate for lessons in the earlier stages of a teaching sequence.

- When appropriate, provide a longer plenary session. Indeed, at the end of a sequence of lessons, you may make over a whole lesson to plenary review. Provide opportunities for pupils to articulate what they have learned, for example:

  - use one of the speaking and listening activities (see pages 10–11) as a means of reviewing what has been learned
  - ask pupils in groups to discuss the text type you have just covered and come up with their own list of key writing points; appoint one member of the group to chair discussion, one to be the secretary who notes the agreed points, and one to be the reporter who feeds back to the class
  - give pairs of children a text-type checklist (see Year 6 page of each text unit) and a published example of the text type to pick holes in.

Major teaching objectives covered in the text units

	Year 3	Year 4	Year 5	Year 6
RECOUNT TEXT	Chronological order **Timelines** Verbs and tense Sequential connectives	Introduction: who, what, when, where? Powerful verbs Word order	Paragraphing Audience and purpose (subjective/objective; personal/impersonal) Reordering sentences	Checklist of organisational and language conventions
REPORT TEXT	**Spidergrams** Formatted reports Sentences and notes Verbs and tense Presentational devices	BOS techniques for spidergrams Organisational devices Notes; key words Descriptive language	Sections and paragraphs Audience and purpose (formal/informal) Comparative reports	Active and passive Checklist of organisational and language conventions
INSTRUCTION TEXT	Organisational and presentational devices Second person verbs	**Flowcharts** Sequential connectives Imperative verbs Statements, questions, commands	Planning, refining, editing for an audience Transforming verbs	Checklist of organisational and language conventions
EXPLANATION TEXT	**Flowcharts** Words essential to meaning	Organisational features Causal connectives and constructions	Spoken/written language Clarity; conciseness	Active and passive Checklist of organisational and language conventions
PERSUASION TEXT		**Pronged bullets** Advertisements Style and vocabulary Connectives to structure an argument	Letter-writing Persuasive devices Presenting persuasion	Framing an argument Checklist of organisational and language conventions
DISCUSSION TEXT				**For-and-against grid** Complex sentences Conditional language Checklist of organisational and language conventions

Recommended books for teachers

Materials from the National Literacy Strategy

Available from Prolog (0845 6022260)

NLS Framework of Objectives (looseleaf folder, 1997) Ref: NLST

Grammar for Writing (book, 2000) (Ref: DfEE 0107/2000)

Developing Early Writing (book, 2001) (Ref: DfEE 0055/2001)

Non-Fiction Writing fliers (six A4 four-page leaflets, 2001)

Available from NLS publications (0118 527531/2)

Reading and Writing Information Texts (Module 6 of the Literacy Training pack, 1998)

(These materials were published by the DfES and distributed to schools in the English state system as part of the National Literacy Strategy. Further copies *may* be available, but in limited numbers.)

Other materials

Skeleton Poster Books (aides memoires for writing) Sue Palmer, TTS Group Limited (01773 830255)

NLS NF Text Level Work Activity Resource Bank, Oxford University Press (01536 741171)

I See What You Mean Steve Moline (Longman Australia) available from Madeleine Lindley Ltd (0161 683 4400)

Visual Tools for Constructing Knowledge David Hyerle, Assoc for Supervision and Curriculum Development, Alexandra, Virginia (www.ascd.org)

Exploring the Writing of Genres Beverley Derewianka, United Kingdom Reading Association (01763 241188)

Writing Frames Maureen Lewis and David Wray, Reading and Language Information Centre (0118 9318820)

Information Texts 1 & 2 (KS1 & KS2) First Steps NLS Edition + associated training, First Steps (Reed Education) (01865 888020)

Teaching Speaking and Listening, KS1 and 2, QCA/99/391 (01787 884444)

The Articulate Classroom: talking and learning in the primary school ed. Prue Goodwin, David Fulton Publishers

Big books that cover specific text types

As books are usually written to convey information, not to teach text types, very few of these are 'perfect examples'. Most are real texts to use in other curricular areas, but to revisit for analysis and discussion when you are teaching the specific text type.

Recount

The First Lunar Landing, Rigby (Magic Bean)

Noah's Ark, CUP (Cambridge Reading)

Historical Letters and Diaries, Longman (Pelican)

Extracts from Zlata's Diary, Heinemann (Literacy World Stage 3 NF)

My Holiday Diary, Heinemann (Discovery World)

Caterpillar Diary, Kingscourt

Writers' Lives, Longman (Pelican)

A Day in the Life of a Storm Chaser, OUP (Literacy Web)

Elizabeth 1/St Francis/Guy Fawkes/Mother Teresa, Heinemann Library (Lives and Times)

Van Gogh/Henry Moore/Joseph Turner, Heinemann Library (Life and Work)

Alan Shearer: a biography, Heinemann (Literacy World Stage 4)

Korky Paul – Biography of an Illustrator, Heinemann (Discovery World)

High Achievers, Rigby (Magic Bean)

Instruction

Round the World Cookbook, Longman (Book Project)

Broomsticks and Balloons, Heinemann (Literacy World Stage 3)

Making Puppets, Rigby (Magic Bean)

Celebration Cook Book, OUP (Literacy Web)

Making Party Decorations, OUP (Literacy Web)

Report

Toads and Their Young, Longman (Book Project)
School by a Volcano (Japan), Longman (Book Project)
Victorian Clothes, Longman (Book Project)
Encyclopaedia of British Wild Animals, Longman (Book Project)
Passenger Ships Now and Fifty Years Ago Longman (Book Project)
Looking After the Egg, Ginn (All Aboard)
Investigating Fungi, Rigby (Magic Bean)
Amazing Landforms, Rigby (Magic Bean)
The Moon, Kingscourt
The Sun, Kingscourt
Zoos Past and Present, Kingscourt
Mathematics from Many Cultures, Kingscourt
Animal Sanctuaries, Kingscourt
Dance, OUP (Oxford Reading Web)
New Year Around the World, OUP (Literacy Web)
The Planets, Heinemann Library
Festivals Through the Year, Heinemann Library
My Christian/Hindu/Muslim Faith, Evans (World Faith Series)
What was it like before electricity?, Evans
Desert, CUP (Cambridge Reading)
Animal Senses, CUP (Cambridge Reading)
Animal Communication, CUP (Cambridge Reading)
A is for Africa, Francis Lincoln

Explanation

Ice Cream, Longman (Book Project)
Water in the House, Longman (Book Project)
Why Jumpers are Woolly, Longman (Book Project)
World Weather, Longman (Pelican)
The Human Body, Longman (Pelican)
A World of Matter, Kingscourt
Exploring Energy, Kingscourt
The Body, BBC (Find Out About)
Broomsticks and Balloons, Heinemann (Literacy World Stage 3)
Spiders and How They Hunt, Heinemann (Literacy World Stage 4)
Quakes and Floods, Heinemann (Literacy World Stage 4)
Wheels and Cranks, Heinemann Library (How It Works)
How Cows Make Milk, Rigby (Magic Bean)
Rainbows, OUP (Literacy Web)

Persuasion

Have Your Say, Heinemann (Literacy World Stage 2)
How To Persuade People, Heinemann (Literacy World Stage 3)

Save Our Earth, Kingscourt
Issues in the News, Longman (Pelican)
Big Issues, Heinemann (Literacy World Stage)
Oxfam/RSPCA/NSPCC/WWF, Heinemann Library (Taking Action Series)

Discussion

Big Issues, Heinemann (Literacy World Stage)
Issues in the News, Longman (Pelican)
Viewpoints on Waste, Rigby (Magic Bean)

Anthologised examples of non-fiction

See publishers' catalogues for contact details.

Non-fiction big books containing examples of several text-types

Own Goal – The Big Book of Football, BBC Educational Publishing
Make Your Own Weather Station, OUP (Oxford Literacy Web)
Tadpole Diary, Kingscourt
What's Cooking, Ginn (All Aboard)
Coastline Journey, Ginn (All Aboard)
Snail, A. & C. Black (Stopwatch)

Big book anthologies

Some of these also cover fiction and poetry.
Literacy Anthology 1 (Y5) & 2 (Y6), Collins (Pathways to Non-Fiction)
Literacy Directions (one for each year of KS2), Ginn
Writing Skills Big Books (one for each year of KS2), Heinemann (Writer's World)
Literacy Line-Up Non-Fiction Big Book, Evans Brothers
Comprehension Success Demonstration Book, OUP
Target Tracker – Writing (Books 3 and 4) CUP

Poster packs and OHTs

Some of these also cover fiction and poetry.
Cornerstones for Writing poster pack and OHTs, Cambridge University Press
Launch into Literacy Demonstration Posters, Oxford University Press
Oxford Literacy Web Poster Packs, Oxford University Press
Models for Writing (OHTs), Ginn

There are now also many sample texts available on the Net, e.g. **bbc.co.uk** (Primary Genie and Xchange).